MIDSOMER MURDERS

THE MAKING OF AN ENGLISH CRIME CLASSIC

JEFF EVANS

BT BATSFORD · LONDON

First Published 2002

Text © Jeff Evans 2002

The right of Jeff Evans to be identified as author of this work has been asserted to him
in accordance with the Copyright, Designs and Patents Act 1988.

Images © Bentley Productions Ltd except pages 45, 46, 47, 50,
51, 109, 151, 154 © Jeff Evans; page 39 © Jim Parker

Volume © B.T. Batsford Ltd 2002

ISBN 07134 8768 2

A CIP catalogue record for this book is available from the British Library.

Typeset in 10/13 Sabon
Printed in Italy by G. Canale & C. S.p.A, Italy
for the publishers

B T Batsford
64 Brewery Road
London N7 9NY
England
www.batsford.com

A member of Chrysalis Books plc

'It is my belief, Watson, founded upon my experience, that the lowest and vilest alleys of London do not present a more dreadful record of sin than does the smiling and beautiful countryside.'

Sherlock Holmes in Sir Arthur Conan Doyle's *The Copper Beeches*.

Acknowledgements

I am extremely grateful to everyone who has made this book possible, from Caroline Graham, who created the characters, to ITV, who wisely commissioned the series from Bentley Productions. Researching this book has been a true pleasure thanks to the co-operation and friendliness of everyone I have needed to contact. The acknowledgements are many, so here goes: a big thank you to John Nettles, Daniel Casey, Brian True-May, Betty Willingale, Jeremy Silberston, Anthony Horowitz, Joyce Nettles, Jim Parker, Christopher Penfold, Jane Wymark, Barry Jackson, Laura Howard, Georgina Hamilton, Colin Skeaping, Ian Strachan, Sarah Hellings, Shelagh Pymm, Gillian Nesbitt and everyone at Bentley for their support, especially Elly Todd for making things happen and putting up with my many queries. At B.T. Batsford, I am grateful to Tina Persaud for her enthusiasm and encouragement. On the domestic front, thanks again to Jacquie, Christopher and Andrew who now hum Jim Parker's theme music in their sleep and can't venture into Oxfordshire or Buckinghamshire without spotting at least one building that has enjoyed its moment of grisly fame as a result of this wonderful TV series.

Jeff Evans

Preface

'Every time I go into a Midsomer village, it's always the same thing: blackmail, sexual deviancy, suicide and murder.'

Detective Chief Inspector Tom Barnaby, Causton CID

In the glorious county of Midsomer, appearances are worryingly deceptive. On the face of it, this is a genteel world of immaculate lace curtains, graceful thatched roofs and roses arcing around the door. Behind the facade, however, the reality is grim. The curtains, crisp and white, are merely a shroud for dark, sighing secrets. The thatch, blonde, cosy and warm, is but the lid on a fiery cauldron of emotions. The roses, red and rambling, may be beautiful but their thorns will draw blood. This is an ambiguous place: homely pots of jam in the larder but rattling skeletons in the cupboard. Charming villages such as Badger's Drift, Midsomer Worthy and Aspern Tallow are delightful communities, home to legions of colourful folk. Most, in the tolerant manner of the English, may be described as cheerfully eccentric but more than a few, it is clear, can only be defined as shockingly psychopathic.

Relaxing events such as the summer fête, cricket on the green, tea on the lawns of a stately home may be blessed with glorious sunshine yet, at the same time, overcast by the black clouds of tragedy. For this little patch of England, chocolate-box pretty and effortlessly green, is no more than a front for homicide of the most gruesome kind. This is the setting for some of the most horrific murders ever conceived. Pitchforks in the abdomen, decapitation by ornamental sword, a burning alive: killings so brutal they make a simple strangulation seem sweet by comparison. Thankfully, the good people of Midsomer have an ally in their fruitless quest for normality.

In the neighbouring town of Causton lives Detective Chief Inspector Barnaby, a calm, reassuring personification of law and order. He is a kind man, a good man, an 'ordinary' man. In this sinister fairground, he alone is capable of throwing the switch that turns off the lights on the grotesque merry-go-round. Midsomer Constabulary is truly lucky to have a man like Barnaby. And should he eventually retire, he will perhaps have groomed a successor to bring calm out of the chaos. Sergeant Gavin Troy does not, it is clear, have the intellectual capabilities of his mentor but the damp patches behind his ears are beginning to dry. Take the chip off his shoulder and he could make a fine detective yet.

Barnaby and Troy are policemen with what might be described as a 'difficult beat'. While the stark streets of the inner city harbour a more obvious threat, the fragrant country lanes of Midsomer are, in reality, a much more frightening prospect. A burly thug with a knuckle-duster for jewellery is no match for a frail old lady with a thirst for revenge. Riots on the streets outside a soccer stadium pale into insignificance next to the fury seething on the courts of a exclusive tennis club. As Barnaby himself admits: 'blackmail, sexual deviancy, suicide and murder', these are the day-to-day problems confronting Causton's law enforcers.

But thankfully this is not reality. This is a fabricated piece of England that draws on every rural stereotype for inspiration, and is so beautifully framed that even murder appears almost acceptable. It is a land pulled from the imagination of novelist Caroline Graham and seamlessly brought to the screen by Bentley Productions. Deaths there may be, but we know this is not the real world. A light touch, a sprinkle of gentle humour, a metaphorical wink at the camera: these ensure viewers know they are in an exaggerated world of make-believe. As colourful as Agatha Christie in her prime, with the mind-bending powers of Conan Doyle, *Midsomer Murders* is detective fiction in a classic tradition.

As colourful as Agatha Christie in her prime, with the mind-bending powers of Conan Doyle, Midsomer Murders *is detective fiction in a classic tradition*

Contents

Foreword by John Nettles   8

1. Introduction   10

2. The Road to Midsomer   12

3. The Birth of Barnaby   19

4. Getting Down to Murder   21

5. The Writer's Tale   28

6. Midsomer Mood Music   38

7. Making Murder Look Easy   40

8. The Real Midsomer   45

9. John Nettles is DCI Barnaby   54

10. Daniel Casey is Sgt Troy   64

11. Jane Wymark is Joyce Barnaby   75

12. Laura Howard is Cully Barnaby   79

13. Barry Jackson is Dr Bullard   82

14. Haven't We Seen You Before?   84

15. Most Welcome Guests   88

16. A Day on the Set   93

17. Episode Guide   95

Index   189

Foreword by John Nettles

When I was but a child my favourite television viewing was the detective series. Everything stopped in our house for *Dixon of Dock Green*; *Maigret* was essential, *Z Cars* a must and anything by Agatha Christie never to be missed. So I jumped at the chance of playing Tom Barnaby in a new series entitled *Midsomer Murders* – for *Midsomer Murders* by Caroline Graham is Agatha Christie on speed!

All the elements of the classic whodunnit are to be found in the tall tales: the bloody murders, the threatened village community full of rural eccentrics, the seemingly inexplicable murders, the shoals of red herrings and, of course, the policeman and his trusty helper, who invariably catch the criminal and solve the mystery – usually by a process of near-magical deduction – to ensure the ultimate triumph of good over evil and the restoration of peace and tranquillity to the small communities. It is a tried and trusted formula and, to judge by the viewing figures, one that still works extraordinarily well.

Detective Chief Inspector Tom Barnaby, who investigates these rural mysteries, is, however, rather a different character from his predecessors in the field in that he is just an ordinary bloke. Not for him exotic personal problems, difficulties with his superiors, concussive contact with the bottle or even a love of classic cars. He loves his work. He's happily married to Joyce and they have a daughter, Cully, with whom they have a perfectly wonderful relationship. In other words, Barnaby is not dysfunctional in any way and that fact alone makes him a highly unusual TV detective! The only irritant in Barnaby's otherwise very pleasant life is Troy, his sidekick, whose laddishness, homophobia and simplistic approach to police work all combine to distress Barnaby mightily – but that is the only cloud in his sky.

The filming of *Midsomer Murders* is not always blessed with good weather but it is always blessed with very fine actors indeed – actors like Richard Briers, Anna Massey, Richard Johnson and Celia Imrie, to name but a few, playing the mad vicars, psychotic spinsters, predatory killers and eccentric busybodies who people the Midsomer world – and also decimate it! The murder rate is, to put it mildly, very high and the killings themselves can be very bloody, to the point where some have had to be toned down or cut for transmission. But, truth to tell, the violence is very far removed from that which occurs in other, more graphic series, like *The Vice*, for example, or *Prime Suspect*. The intention is to entertain, thrill and often amuse the viewer, to make the programme as enjoyable to watch as the production team and I find it to make.

John Nettles

Introduction

The origins of *Midsomer Murders* lie in 1987, with the publication of the novel *The Killings at Badger's Drift* by Century Hutchinson. Caroline Graham's first whodunnit was immediately acclaimed and voted one of the top 100 crime novels of all time by the Crime Writers' Association. The world she created – a timeless land of picture-postcard English villages inhabited by colourful eccentrics – clearly drew on the success of Agatha Christie several decades earlier. But her tongue-in-cheek approach and quirky humour placed Graham's writing in a different league. 'Agatha Christie on speed' is one popular description of Caroline's style.

Ten years later, Inspector Barnaby made the leap from the written page to the television screen. It was a quiet time in the UK for detective dramas. Inspector Morse, the king of the cerebral cops, had for the most part laid down his crown. Ruth Rendell's Reg Wexford had retired to his Hampshire home, and P D James's Adam Dalgliesh was doing much the same in East Anglia. Taggart, despite the death of its leading man, was grinding on in the grim streets of Glasgow, while Jack Frost was battling with urban crime in fictional Denton. However, for a country copper there was a glaring vacancy. Tom Barnaby easily fitted the bill.

Finding a star to fill Barnaby's shiny shoes was not difficult. The advert might have read: 'Wanted: mature actor with a loyal following', but there was no need to advertise. John Nettles was an obvious choice. A decade as Jersey cop Jim Bergerac had made Nettles a household name but five subsequent years on stage with the Royal Shakespeare Company had laid down enough distance to enable John to return to television as a new, notably different, police officer.

The pilot episode, 'The Killings at Badger's Drift', was cautiously described as a one-off film and broadcast by ITV on Sunday, 23 March 1997. Much was made of John Nettles's return to prime time, but viewers expecting Bergerac mark II soon realized that Barnaby was not the same copper at all. This was no Channel Islands tearaway, battling against booze addiction, struggling with a bad leg and falling out with a succession of girlfriends. Now Nettles was surrounded by suburbia, comforted by his loving wife and daughter, and patrolling a patch of tranquil England. In place of leather bomber jackets there were Marks & Spencer three-piece suits; instead of a flashy 1940s Triumph, a practical blue Mondeo. From being largely a lone operator like Bergerac,

Barnaby was now part of a duo, joined in his investigations by a young, keen, but notably immature sergeant named Troy. Viewers liked it and Nettles was an instant hit. Despite competing with BBC 1's hugely popular police series *Hamish Macbeth*, the film attracted a massive 13.5 million viewers. A series just had to follow.

A year later, the four remaining Barnaby novels were adapted for the small screen, attracting an average audience figure of 10 million – in a multi-channel age, with competition from the revitalized cinema and countless other leisure possibilities, this was an extremely healthy and remarkably consistent total. And viewing figures continued to hold up for later episodes that took Barnaby away from his creator, with new plots written specifically for television.

Similar success followed around the world, as *Midsomer Murders* gathered fans in countries as varied as Albania and Venezuela. In the USA, the programme has been screened by the A&E network to millions of loyal viewers who indulge themselves on a sumptuous diet of English stereotypes – thatched cottages, village fêtes, red telephone boxes and wacky country folk.

But leaving aside its central character and its picturesque settings, there are other powerful reasons for the series' success. That 'other-worldliness' for a start. Viewers recognize that *Midsomer Murders* is the television equivalent of a classic detective novel, a far-fetched yarn, a good old-fashioned whodunnit that provides instant escapism. Then there are the guest stars, some of them giants of British stage and screen, whose presence raises every episode into near feature film status. Not least, there is the mood – the feeling that everything is not quite as charming as it appears. With a block on time – 'spiritually it's in the '50s', says John Nettles – the programme celebrates, according to its star, 'a certain form of Englishness – a rather beautiful place that we like to think has existed but never really has.'

> *Midsomer Murders is the television equivalent of a classic detective novel, a far-fetched yarn, a good old-fashioned whodunnit that provides instant escapism.*

The Road to Midsomer

'English villages where things are not always what they seem. If you bend to sniff a rose, a worm may come out'

When you've a new production company to establish, you need plenty of ideas. That's the situation in which Brian True-May found himself with the launch of Bentley Productions in the mid-1990s. It was handy, therefore, to have a friend and former colleague such as Betty Willingale to consult. Brian asked Betty if she could come up with some projects. They had worked together on an Andrew Davies drama called *Harnessing Peacocks*, which had won Gold and Silver Nymph awards at Cannes, with Brian the associate producer and Betty taking care of script and casting. They followed this with the dramatization of another Mary Wesley novel called *The Vacillations of Poppy Carew* for Meridian. Now, Betty, a veteran of BBC period dramas such as *Mansfield Park* and *Fortunes of War*, had taken a liking to Caroline Graham's Inspector Barnaby novels and suggested to Brian that they would make ideal television fare.

'I thought the novels were very funny,' she recalls. 'They were old-fashioned, "body in the library" detective stories, with no car chases or brawls. At the time, there were an awful lot of crash-bang-wallop police series on TV but not much in the way of middle-of-the-road detective stories. I also liked the fact that the central character was a happily married policeman with a nice wife and daughter. There were five novels we could dramatize and then I felt we could have writers providing new plots for the characters.'

The BBC was no longer making *Miss Marple*, possibly the nearest thing to *Midsomer Murders*, so Betty could see a gap in the schedules. She asked Brian to look at Caroline's books and he agreed that *The Killings at Badger's Drift*, in particular, would work well on television. They decided to share the workload to get the project off the ground. 'He asked me to produce,' recalls Betty, 'but I really didn't want to do the day-to-day producing chores, so we split the job.'

The result was that Brian took care of what Betty calls 'the yelling to get things done' and looked after the money, while she focused on 'the artistic bit', handling scripts, casting and music.

Betty pulled together a team of people with whom she could work. Director Jeremy Silberston she had known for years at the BBC, when he worked with her as production assistant on serials such as *Bleak House* and *Smiley's People*. He had just branched out into directing and Betty saw *Midsomer Murders* as the perfect springboard for his talents. 'I thought it was good to have a director who was really ready to fly,' she explains. 'I knew he could do it and he took it with both hands.' Jeremy remembers how he and Betty set the tone for the series. 'We approached the pilot wanting to keep the essence of Caroline Graham's novels, creating a world that is slightly parallel to reality, but avoiding modernity – we didn't want lots of fast cars, for instance.' Anthony Horowitz, who had worked with Betty on *Agatha Christie's Poirot*, was chosen as the first scriptwriter and, in Jeremy's words, 'provided a cracking screenplay'. 'Anthony was marvellous,' agrees Betty. 'He kept the spirit of the novels but made the characters his own. He's got the right humour, he's terribly good at plotting and when he comes up with suggestions like killing off a vicar or having a murder committed in the middle of a cricket match, you know it will work.'

Award-winning composer Jim Parker, with whom Jeremy had collaborated on *The House of Eliott*, was then brought on board to establish the soundtrack, and

A happy crew: the team behind 'The Killings at Badger's Drift'.

Derek Bain was added as editor. 'Jim was hugely important in developing the style and tone of the series', confirms Jeremy, while Betty declares Derek to be 'brilliant'. 'He's got a sensitive ear and eye to the needs of the series,' she says.

Caroline Graham was involved a little in her novels' transition to television but largely allowed the Bentley team to adopt and adapt her characters. It was immediately decided, however, that Barnaby should continue to be a nice man, as in the books. 'He's our storyteller,' explains Betty. 'He takes the audience by the hand and they follow his reasoning. But he needs to be involved and brought into the action.'

Brian confirms that it was a conscious decision to bring Barnaby much more into the stories than he had been in Caroline's books. 'British television is not terribly keen on films where there is no thread or strand – no major actor or personality of some sort,' he says, explaining how the search began for an actor to fill Barnaby's boots. 'We always thought that we needed a leading actor that could look mature and sensible and not some sort of young whippersnapper who wouldn't have fitted the role that Caroline had set out. John Nettles was our favourite choice and I'd been up to Stratford to see him. Since *Bergerac*, he'd matured and he looked the part.' For Betty, too, John Nettles was the obvious choice. He wasn't what might be called one of the hot stars of the moment, but after ten years as Bergerac he had a big, loyal following – a housewives' favourite, if you like.

Brian went to see ITV's controller of drama, Nick Elliott, and told him they wanted John to play the lead, but Elliott suggested the late Michael Williams instead. 'I had lunch with Michael, who was a charming man,' recalls Brian, 'but, sadly, I felt he was too old. If the series was going to run for years he would have been past his retirement age. So Betty and I stuck to our guns and they gave in and let us go with John Nettles.'

> *'I loved this idea of an imaginary county, where the location was the hero, not the detective.'*

Daniel Casey, who had recently been seen in the enormously successful *Our Friends in the North*, was auditioned and cast as Sgt Troy. But this was a quite different Troy from the spiteful, sexist character created for the books. 'We thought making Troy as unpleasant as he is in the novels would not work on television. It would become boring,' reveals Betty. As a result, the TV Troy is much more personable and enthusiastic.

However, one aspect of Caroline's novels that just had to be retained was the setting. Betty loved the idea of 'English villages where things are not always what they seem. If you bend to sniff a rose, a worm may come out'. It was a deliberate decision to keep story lines within this tight setting as much as possible. 'In the first episode we needed to film some scenes in Brighton, so we took a day out', explains Betty. 'But we weren't keen on that. As soon as you step out of this "never never land" you weaken the series.' However, safe in fictitious Midsomer, Bentley soon realized they could afford to take more than a few liberties with the truth. 'In our setting we can be outrageous,' says Betty. 'We have some of the most gruesome murders but it's not really frightening for viewers because they know it's not true. Played with a bit of a laugh, it is very palatable.' The absence of graphic action makes this possible. 'We keep away from violence,' adds Brian. 'Violence is graphic only in the imagination.' He recalls the first episode when a key character was stabbed to death. 'The stage directions called for blood all over the walls and ceiling, and that's exactly how it was shot, but it looked horrendous so it had to be re-done.'

To remove the series further from reality, authentic police procedure was purposely avoided from the start. 'Barnaby does occasionally call in the scene of crimes unit, or interviews somebody at the station,' Betty explains, 'but the rule is: As little police procedure as possible. We didn't even want Barnaby to have a shouting boss, like Inspector Morse or Jack Frost. This way we have more scope for fun. And because we have nothing to do with current affairs or the outside world, we're not hamstrung. This is not cutting edge: it is escapism. Watching *Midsomer Murders* is like reading a good detective story. There is no social comment.'

Betty was also influential in devising the structure of the series, particularly when it came to how each story was explained to the viewer. 'I took an executive decision not to flinch from the flashback,' she reveals. 'In these stories, it is often something that has happened in the past that causes horror in the present. Also, it is important that viewers see the murders happen: they don't see who did it, but they see how it happened. We then use flashbacks to reveal the killers later, and this allows us to avoid having Barnaby gathering everyone together at the end to explain how it all happened. We do it visually.'

When it came to a title for the new series, a little head scratching was required before Anthony Horowitz delivered the goods. 'If I have one claim to fame in my life it is that I came up with the title *Midsomer Murders* – or, in my version, *The Midsomer Murders*,' he says. Anthony remembers that, when he was approached to write for the series, the title that had been pencilled in was simply 'Barnaby'. 'The very first thing I said was that it was absolutely wrong to have a one-word title,' he explains. 'Barnaby was not the hero of these programmes: Midsomer was.' It has been widely reported that Anthony suggested the name of the series after a weekend away in the West Country, where he visited the village of Midsomer Norton. However, the truth is that Anthony had just visited his friend and writing mentor Richard Carpenter, who lives at Ayot St Peter – one of a couple of 'Ayot' villages in Hertfordshire – and came back thinking that it would be good to emulate this by having lots of 'Midsomer' villages, set in a fictitious county. 'I loved this idea of an imaginary county,' Anthony declares, 'where the location was the hero, not the detective.' The first book he was looking to adapt, *Written in Blood*, had been set by Caroline Graham in the village of Midsomer Worthy. 'Hence Midsomer Murders,' he says.

Meanwhile talks continued to find an outlet for the series. Brian approached Carlton Television who were very keen but came back with a deal that wasn't attractive. Then the media group Chrysalis offered to buy into Brian's company and was prepared to put up half a million pounds towards running and developing it. This gave Brian the opportunity to explore a new 'licence deal' that ITV had introduced.

The arrangement works a little like taking out a mortgage. Producers with an idea develop it at their own expense and sell the idea to ITV. A price is negotiated

Barnaby and Troy – 'Badger's Drift' vintage.

and the producer borrows money from a bank to make the film. When it is delivered, ITV pays the money and repayment is made to the bank, hopefully leaving a comfortable profit for the production company. 'We were one of the very first people to do this,' explains Brian, 'and since then a lot of independents have followed.' Brian concedes that the Chrysalis connection came in very handy, as spending hundreds of thousands of pounds on development is a risky business for a small operator.

ITV duly gave the go-ahead, a pilot episode, 'The Killings at Badger's Drift', was made and Yorkshire Television was brought in as the compliance agency – a regulatory requirement to guarantee that the content and the technical merits of a programme are up to the necessary standards for broadcast. These hurdles jumped and hoops negotiated, Brian and Betty were immediately rewarded with a success. 'The Killings at Badger's Drift' went out on 23 March 1997 and was a massive hit, notching up 13.5 million viewers. 'They decided to repeat it four months later and it attracted 12 million viewers,' a thrilled Brian recalls. 'In fact, it's since been repeated yet again and got 6.8 million – on New Year's Eve, when everyone was partying.'

The success of the pilot was particularly exciting for Daniel Casey. 'I thought "Badger's Drift" was an excellent episode. It had such a good cast and it was the first thing John had done since *Bergerac*. There was great interest in whether it was going to be similar, being another detective series. But you could see as soon as it was made that it was perfect fare for a series. We got the biggest figures for any single drama that year. It was huge.'

Understandably, a series was soon commissioned and arrived just over a year later with Anthony Horowitz's adaptation of *Written in Blood*. With 23 screened episodes and more on the way, *Midsomer Murders* is now widely recognized as a solid brick in the wall of British television drama and the start of each new season is an eagerly anticipated event.

The Bentley Story

The success of Bentley, or at least the speed of it, seems to have taken Brian True-May by surprise. Brian set up as a freelancer after working for ATV (latterly Central/Carlton) for 21 years, only leaving when his job as production manager was relocated from Elstree Studios to Nottingham. One of the last big productions he worked on was the original *Auf Wiedersehen, Pet*.

'I was offered a job in Nottingham and I didn't want to go,' he remembers. 'This forced me to go on my own.' Ironically, his first freelance job then took him straight to Nottingham to work for Central, making a series about the rag trade called *Connie*, which starred Stephanie Beacham. He admits to never really thinking about making his own programmes at the time and was mainly working with a producer called Malcolm Craddock. 'It was mostly for Channel 4 in those days – independents didn't make much on location for the main ITV companies or the BBC,' he says. Malcolm has since become well-known for producing the *Sharpe* series and Brian nearly joined him. 'I was about to go to the Crimea for five months to do *Sharpe* when Meridian Television came along. They needed someone with my experience to work on a drama called *Harnessing Peacocks* because the production company making it had never produced anything before.'

Thus began Brian's working relationship with Betty Willingale which was eventually to lead to *Midsomer Murders*. 'After *Harnessing Peacocks*, I was

> *'Violence is graphic only in the imagination.'*

commissioned to make *The Vacillations of Poppy Carew*,' he explains. Brian already had a company which he called Smith and Jones Productions. It was basically a front for him to 'do a little bit of moonlighting' when he was at Central Television, and was named after the *Alias Smith and Jones* Western series. Sharing the name was a location catering company that Brian's wife used to run. 'I had five kitchen units going all over the country on location, mainly for the BBC,' he reveals. After *Poppy Carew*, Brian started work on the wrestling

comedy, *Rumble*, and, as he puts it, 'was scratching around for other bits and pieces on the side to make the money up'. He'd also worked earlier with Mick Pilsworth at Alomo Productions, as executive in charge of production on *Birds of a Feather* and *Love Hurts*. Mick had moved on to the Chrysalis media group and one day phoned Brian out of the blue to say Chrysalis wanted to invest in his business. But they needed to change the company name. 'We wanted to think of a name that was synonymous with high quality, but one that is very recognizable,' says Brian. They considered Jaguar Productions and Rolls-Royce Productions before arriving at Bentley.

On set: John Nettles with Brian True-May.

Once Bentley was established, Chrysalis injected half a million pounds. Two years later, Chrysalis agreed to give Brian another half a million, even though he didn't have anything in production at the time, but in the end they didn't need to. 'About a week or two later, I got the commission for 'The Killings at Badger's Drift' and never looked back,' he says.

Eventually, Chrysalis bought Brian out completely to take over the company. While he now belongs to a large corporation, he still enjoys a great deal of independence. 'I'm very much a one-man band with my team of three girls,' he explains and underlines how the deal has been good for both him and Chrysalis. 'The catalogue of *Midsomer Murders* must be worth millions, so they've done all right and I'm quite happy to carry on while they leave me alone to get on with it.'

While *Midsomer Murders* continues in full flow, Bentley has broadened its horizons, producing the Ross Kemp SAS drama *Ultimate Force* and now developing another series called *Nightmare City*, a big action, police, crime-corruption series set in Blackpool. 'To get two major series commissioned from ITV is quite remarkable,' says Brian. But there's no lack of commitment to *Midsomer Murders*. 'While the figures keep up, and I'm sure we shall keep them up, there's no reason why it can't continue.'

The Birth of Barnaby

In 1987 gentle spinster Emily Simpson was murdered in her own home. The crime was heinous, the man charged with finding the killer was Detective Chief Inspector Tom Barnaby. It was the first the world had heard of this likeable, avuncular copper as he made his debut in Caroline Graham's first novel, *The Killings at Badger's Drift*. Barnaby was an immediate success and five more novels featuring Causton's finest lawman have since followed. It was only a matter of time before Caroline's hero made the cross-medium leap into the world of television.

Born in Warwickshire, Caroline Graham enjoyed a varied career before taking up her pen. She worked as a dancer and an actress – hence the strong theatrical slant to her writing – also serving in the Women's Royal Naval Service and managing a marriage bureau for a while. Following the birth of a son, she turned to writing and freelance broadcasting, anticipating her future involvement with television by scripting several episodes of the daily soap *Crossroads*.

Building on the success of *The Killings at Badger's Drift*, Caroline's follow-up novel, *Death of a Hollow Man*, a tale of bitter rivalries in an amateur theatre group, was released in 1989, with *Death in Disguise*, set in a New Age commune, published in 1992. *Written in Blood*, released in 1994, was a mystery wrapped around a village writing group, while *Faithful Unto Death*, in 1996, took kidnap as its central theme. Caroline also wrote the screenplay for 'Death of a Hollow Man', once Barnaby had transferred to television.

For the actors filling the roles created by Caroline, the books have provided useful background information, although, because the characters have all been adapted in some way for television, the actors have to be wary about how

Creator and creations: Caroline Graham with Barnaby and Troy.

closely they follow Caroline's descriptions. Daniel Casey confirms this. 'You treat them as two separate things: one is a piece of literature and one is a piece of television, but I think it was important to read the books to see the kind of world these people inhabited. I read three or four of them straight away. They've got a lovely, quirky nature and Caroline's got a fantastic imagination. The novels are also very dark and we've really fought to keep that dark element in the series.'

> *'They've got a lovely, quirky nature ... the novels are also very dark and we've really fought to keep that dark element in the series.'*

Graham's most recent Barnaby novel is *A Place of Safety*, the only one so far published since the start of the TV series, although Bentley has no plans to adapt the book for the small screen. In 1999, the same year as *A Place of Safety* was released, Caroline also penned a short Inspector Barnaby story for the *Daily Mail*. Published in two parts, beginning on Christmas Eve, it was another dip into the world of the Causton theatre and its troupe of egotistic amateur players. A shambolic performance of Dickens's *A Christmas Carol*, witnessed by Tom, Joyce and Cully Barnaby, Cully's boyfriend, Nico, and Troy, takes a sinister turn for the worse and it looks like Joyce's perfect family Christmas may once again be under threat.

Caroline has also written children's books and two other crime novels which do not feature Inspector Barnaby: *Murder at Madingley Grange* and *The Envy of a Stranger*.

A Place of Safety

Ferne Basset is the setting for Caroline Graham's latest foray behind the twitching lace curtains of Midsomer. The village, 12 miles from Causton, is home to Lionel Lawrence, a retired vicar who provides shelter and encouragement for wayward youths. When one of these troublesome teenagers vanishes one night, Barnaby and Troy find themselves tangled in a complex web of murder and blackmail. Key characters include Lionel's subjugated wife, Ann; her friend, former financial broker Louise Fainlight; Louise's brother, Valentine, a homosexual writer of children's books; the Lawrences' daily, Hetty Leathers, and her abusive husband, Charlie; village confidante Evadne Peat; and Lionel's slimy chauffeur, Jax. Once again, we have ample proof that a Midsomer village is really the last place in which one should feel safe.

Getting Down to Murder

Keeping up standards is paramount in Brian True-May's mind when he sets about producing a new series of *Midsomer Murders*. 'We make sure the quality is absolutely tip-top', he declares, and to this end commits £1.25 million to each episode. 'That has to include not just the cost of making it, but all the development, all the overheads, the cost of insurance and interest on the borrowed money.' It is, however, the artists' budget which runs up the biggest expenditure (nearly 20 per cent of the overall budget), largely because of the calibre of the guest stars. 'If you've got someone like Richard Briers, he's expensive,' admits Brian. 'But bloody good, too!'

The art department usually accounts for another chunk of money, as do make-up and wardrobe, because the clothes the actors wear tend to be all new – not necessarily designer gear, but quality country clothing. Day-to-day responsibility for keeping costs under control falls to Ian Strachan, Brian's associate producer. Brian now sees his own job rather as a chief executive, making sure he has the right people doing the right jobs across the board, but he still has a say if the budget looks stretched. 'When it comes to scripts, I might read a story line and say we can't afford to do this. This hasn't really happened on *Midsomer Murders* although some episodes can be very expensive because we've had a lot of actors and extras in them. But in a run of five shows, number two might be quite heavy but number three might be quite light, so they generally even themselves out in cost.'

Making the films is a major logistical exercise. Around 65 people make up the film unit on average, but on some days this can swell to about 120. 'It's an

> *'the runner/drivers have to go and pick up artists sometimes at 5.30. They bring them to the set, they have a bit of breakfast, do their make-up and costume and then we're on camera at 8, finishing at 7 at night.'*

At work in the woods: the team prepares to shoot a scene from 'Death of a Stranger'.

enormous set-up,' says Brian adding up the number of trucks, trailers and people who provide the backup facilities. 'It's exactly the same as a feature film. The only difference with *Midsomer Murders* is that we're shooting on Super 16 film not 35mm, and obviously we have less to spend, but otherwise the operation's exactly the same.' Sometimes there are two camera units in action. 'We may have complicated scenes to film with the main actors and there are sequences involving a car chase or a stunt that need shooting, so we'll send a second unit away with stunt doubles in the cars – you can't really see who they are – and film them with another camera crew.'

Each film takes five weeks to complete. 'We allow between 24 and 26 days to shoot the principal photography and we work on the basis of 11-day fortnights, so as not to kill everybody off,' Brian laughs. 'We used to do a six-day week but it was just too much because of the hours. First call for make-up is usually 7 am, so the runner/drivers have to go and pick up artists sometimes at 5.30. They bring them to the set, they have a bit of breakfast, do their make-up and costume and then we're on camera at 8, finishing at 7 at night. It's a long day. So at least they now get alternate weekends off.'

It's a tiring process, as Daniel Casey confirms. 'I get home about 8 o'clock, then I do an hour, or an hour-and-a-half, on my script after work. You can't go out during the week because you just can't function the next day, but we do have a two-week break in the summer.'

In the Bleak Midsomer

Compared to other series, Brian True-May doesn't see *Midsomer Murders* as being a problematical series to make. 'If anything, it's relatively easy,' he says. 'I suppose the only problem we get, because it's *Midsomer Murders* and there's a pun on 'midsummer', is that we want to make it look sunny and pretty, but many a time we've had bad days. Twice, I remember, we've been filming fêtes, where it's been raining and freezing cold. On one occasion, because the light wasn't too bad, the artists had assistants holding umbrellas over their heads. At the very last minute, they pulled the umbrella away, shot the scene and then put the umbrellas back again before all the hair got wet. On another occasion, we were filming a fête and it was raining, so we let people wear macs and carry umbrellas. It looked fine.'

Director Jeremy Silberston has similar memories. 'The summer we filmed "Dead Man's Eleven" was particularly rainy,' he says, 'and we kept having to stop the cricket scenes and go inside. The budget is not large enough for us to wait for the weather. Luckily, we did have plenty of interior scenes to do while it was pouring down. There's one scene where Robert Hardy is urging his team on in the dressing room but outside it was actually bucketing down.'

Ironically, when rain is required by the script, it has to be faked. Unexpected rain can, however, be a bonus, as stunt co-ordinator Colin Skeaping reveals. 'We had one sequence where some schoolboys were swimming in a lake and a body rises out of the water. I think we had the worst day's weather of the year. It absolutely bucketed down. In the end we did it in the pouring rain and terrible light and went home thinking we were going to have to re-shoot it. But when we saw it, it actually was a bonus: it lent an atmosphere to the sequence. It made it spooky.'

Filming on the series begins in mid-May and runs through until mid-November, so rain is not the only potential weather hazard. Once a barbecue at Little Marlow was threatened by low temperatures. 'We arrived in the morning and we had white frost,' remembers Brian. 'We could avoid looking at the ground too much but, of course, the actors were freezing and there was vapour

The Barnabys can't resist a good fête – in fair weather or foul.

coming out of their mouths. So, for close ups, we asked them to suck on an ice cube for a few seconds before saying their lines. You don't get any vapour then.' Fog has also presented difficulties. 'We did a scene on a bowling green when we had fog,' says Brian. 'We started to shoot but it was hopeless, so we had to do that again.'

The Funny Side of Murder

'We have a lot of fun', says John Nettles about the ups and downs of filming *Midsomer Murders*. As programmes like *It'll Be Alright on the Night* prove time and again, not everything goes to plan in the world of TV production. John remembers one particular bloomer that caused much mirth on the set. 'It was when I knocked on a door and announced myself as "Detective Sergeant Bergerac" by mistake,' he laughs. 'They never let me live that one down.'

A barbecue at Little Marlow was threatened by low temperatures ... 'the actors were freezing and there was vapour coming out of their mouths ... we asked them to suck on an ice cube for a few seconds before saying their lines. You don't get any vapour then.'

His co-star recalls another slip of John's tongue that had the crew in stitches. 'In 'Strangler's Wood', John had to look through three files for the girls that had been murdered,' says Daniel Casey. 'One of the girls was called Joan Chaplin, but John accidentally called her "Joan Collins". It was my close up and out of the corner of my eye I saw the cameraman's shoulder start to shake. John was absolutely oblivious. I kept telling myself to concentrate and not to look. When they finally called "cut", all of us burst out laughing'. Daniel had to explain to John that he had just finished off one of our biggest stars. *Midsomer Murders* may be a pretty ruthless show but it's going a bit far when, as Daniel says, 'Joan Collins hadn't even been in it and was killed off.'

Sometimes the boot is on the other foot, however. 'My first day on the show was hilarious,' Daniel concedes. 'My first scene with John had us driving to the murder scene. We had to drive up to the police activity, get out of the car, have a little "conflab" over the car and walk in.' Daniel duly pulled up in the car, got out and turned round, but there was no John. 'I'd parked inches away from a bollard and John just couldn't get out,' he laughs. 'I'd only known him three days and I'd already upstaged him hugely. But every day there's something funny going on.'

Midsomer Mother

For writer Anthony Horowitz, one figure stands out as the guiding light in the creation of *Midsomer Murders*: producer Betty Willingale. 'Betty is one of these people who has been in British television for as long as anybody can remember,' he says in a way that is appreciative of, and grateful for, the way in which she has collected talented individuals like himself during her career and groomed them as her protégés. 'It's like she is a ship going through the waters of television in a stately procession, picking up various people along the way, and never really putting them down.' Another tribute comes from Brian True-May. 'Once the BBC used to be described as "Auntie",' he says. 'It was a very endearing term and Betty sums up that image of Auntie. She's the original BBC – in the way she looks and in her incredible encyclopaedic knowledge of writers, actors and everything creative.'

The sound of the chase: an engineer runs with hounds during the filming of 'Death of a Stranger'.

Betty worked for the BBC right through the glory days of the 1960s, 1970s and 1980s, at a time when its reputation for drama was being established. She began on the popular soap opera *Compact*, moving on to numerous adaptations of literary classics that brightened Britain's living rooms every Sunday teatime. Later came such notable series as *I, Claudius* and *Tinker, Tailor, Soldier, Spy* (as script editor) as well as the acclaimed *Fortunes of War*, which she produced. Her experience is widely recognized and her judgement,

'I knocked on a door and announced myself as "Detective Sergeant Bergerac" by mistake.'

particularly in casting and scriptwork, universally trusted. Betty was producer of the first three series of *Midsomer Murders*, and, although now largely retired, is still employed as a consultant by Bentley.

Midsomer Murders Directors

Jeremy Silberston

*Awaiting the
director's call
on the set for
'Market for
Murder'.*

'The Killings at Badger's Drift'; 'Written in Blood'; 'Death of a Hollow Man'; 'Death's Shadow'; 'Strangler's Wood'; 'Dead Man's Eleven'; 'Judgement Day'; 'Dark Autumn'

The first *Midsomer Murders* director, Jeremy Silberston began with the BBC and has directed some of the best known programmes on British television, including *Casualty*, *The Bill*, *Brookside*, *EastEnders* and *The House of Eliott*. He has since collaborated with writer Anthony Horowitz on ITV's period crime drama, *Foyle's War*.

Baz Taylor

'Faithful Unto Death'; 'Death in Disguise'

Baz Taylor is a vastly experienced director who has worked on some truly memorable series. These include *Shine On Harvey Moon*, *Shabby Tiger*, *Auf Wiedersehen, Pet*, *Strangers*, *Bergerac*, *Birds of a Feather*; *Lovejoy*, *Crocodile Shoes*, *The Bill*, *Heartbeat*, *Minder*, *El C.I.D.*, and, more recently, *My Family*.

Moira Armstrong

'Blood Will Out'; 'Beyond the Grave'

Over a long career, which began in the 1960s, Moira Armstrong has directed countless major TV dramas, including *The Troubleshooters*, *Z Cars*, *Adam Adamant Lives!*, *The Guardians*, *Budgie*, *Freud*, *Bluebell*, *Beryl's Lot*, *Body and Soul*, *Boon*, *All for Love*, *Testament of Youth* and *Hazell*.

Peter Cregeen

'Death of a Stranger'
A prolific director/producer, Peter Cregeen has made his name through work on such notable series as *Out of the Unknown*, *The Onedin Line*, *Colditz*, *Wings*, *Nanny*, *The Gentle Touch*, *The Choir* and *The Bill*.

Peter Smith

'Blue Herrings'; 'Garden of Death'; 'The Electric Vendetta'; 'Tainted Fruit'; 'Murder on St Malley's Day'
Peter Smith's directing career has covered three decades, from programmes such as *The Sweeney*, *Target* and *Shoestring* in the 1970s, through *The Price*, *A Perfect Spy*, *Resnick*, *Between the Lines*, *A Touch of Frost* and *Seaforth* in the 1980s and 1990s, to *Midsomer Murders* in the new millennium.

David Tucker

'Destroying Angel'; 'Who Killed Cock Robin?'; 'A Worm in the Bud'
Diana, *Tenko*, *Miss Marple*, *A Very Peculiar Practice*, *The Gravy Train*, *A Year in Provence*, *Stanley and the Women*, *Bramwell*, *Rhinoceros* and *A&E* are just some of the major dramas that benefited from David Tucker's direction before he joined the *Midsomer Murders* team.

Sarah Hellings

'Ring Out Your Dead'; 'Market for Murder'
Sarah Hellings has directed a variety of top British drama series, including *Doctor Who*, *Boon*, *Lovejoy*, *Forever Green*, *The Memoirs of Sherlock Holmes*, *Catherine Cookson's The Glass Virgin* and *Lucy Sullivan is Getting Married*.

The Writer's Tale

The road to a new *Midsomer Murders* episode begins with the script, which is where Christopher Penfold comes in. Penfold is one of the country's leading writers and script editors, having worked on series such as *Space: 1999*, *All Creatures Great and Small*, *Casualty* and *The Bill*. A few years ago, he founded ScriptWorks, a loose association of the country's top script editors, to provide a script development service for producers. When Betty Willingale decided to step down as producer of *Midsomer Murders*, she recommended Christopher as her replacement script editor.

Red herrings are deliberately strewn throughout the story line to send viewers up a blind alley

Christopher's job involves choosing the writers and discussing possible story lines with them. He shows them the series 'Bible' – a detailed style guide illustrating the dos and don'ts of writing for the series. They watch earlier episodes and Christopher ensures they know the direction to follow.

'The writer then goes away and comes back with a story line,' Christopher explains. 'If we like it, we ask him to develop it into a longer proposal, which is then seen by producer Brian True-May.' Brian reveals that there are numerous fallers at this first hurdle and that one of the biggest problems is finding story lines that are suitably different from what has gone before. 'We've had a couple recently that look like jigsaw puzzles of all the previous episodes put together, with nothing fresh,' he says.

Story line agreed, however, the next stage is to commission a treatment. This is a long, 20–30-page document in which the writer works out every step of the plot. It is a daunting piece of work, as Christopher reveals. 'Not all writers are sympathetic to this process but *Midsomer Murders* is complicated in that it is an elaborately plotted whodunnit with good, eccentric characterization. The success of the series stems from the way in which it actively engages the audience in solving the whodunnit. So, in the treatment, we need to get the structure right. We have to line up all the suspects and red herrings, and plot all the twists and turns which allow Barnaby to put the facts together and solve the crime.' Although there is a lot of work in preparing a treatment, it is a necessary step along the way towards ensuring *Midsomer Murders* works. 'To run a main story line through with lots of sub-plots is an intricate, mechanical thing that not everybody can do,' says Brian. 'They get themselves into a muddle.'

The treatment is shown to ITV and, if they like it, a first draft of the script is commissioned. When this is delivered Christopher and others go through it making notes and suggestions. 'I collate all the comments for a script meeting with the writer, which usually takes all day,' he says. 'The writer then prepares a second draft, which is hopefully nearer the mark. The director and casting director might see this. Once the plot has been tightened, it is in this second draft that the writer can loosen up and develop characters, but some writers manage to make characters jump off the page in the treatment.'

Writers also have an input into the casting. With writer and director getting together fairly early in the production process, there is an opportunity to explore what the writer has in mind regarding actors. Some writers have thought about the performers they'd want in the roles, but others simply concentrate on writing the characters and leave the rest to the casting department. Anthony Horowitz, for instance, remembers pencilling in Timothy West for the part of Marcus Devere in 'Judgement Day', but admits he generally waits for the casting director to find the right actors to fill the roles he creates.

Timothy West: an obvious choice for Anthony Horowitz in 'Judgement Day'.

The choice of writers is vital to the success of the series. 'I try to introduce one or two new writers each year,' says Christopher, 'to provide new voices and keep things fresh.' Even so, the writers are all experienced – names inked in for the next series include Alan Plater and P J Hammond – but not all find the format easy to handle and some fall by the wayside. 'Some understand *Midsomer Murders* quickly, but others never get it at all,' Christopher explains. 'It's a really difficult act. Sustaining two hours is a tall order – every episode is basically a feature film. In a lot of long TV dramas, the story is stretched out to fill the time, but I try to pack the narrative. In fact, one way to pull the wool over the audience's eyes is to keep moving the story along so they can't keep up.'

Each *Midsomer Murders* episode is divided into six parts. The first part takes the form of a programme teaser, which introduces an air of mystery and intrigue and culminates in a murder. This is followed by the title sequence. In the next part, Barnaby and Troy are brought in as soon as possible to get the story

Writer and son: Anthony Horowitz with his son Cassian, who appeared in 'Judgement Day'.

moving, before another murder or dramatic highpoint at the end of this section. Similar climaxes follow at the end of other sections as the episode nears its conclusion. Every effort is made to ensure the involvement of the viewing audience in the detection process, and red herrings are deliberately strewn throughout the story line to send viewers up a blind alley. Much attention is devoted to characterization, the creation of larger than life personalities that not only enhance the story line but give the casting department plenty of scope for attracting major guest performers.

Although the series Bible lays down some golden rules, flexibility is allowed from time to time. 'The Bible changes from year to year and all rules are there to be broken,' says Christopher. The use of the flashback is a good example. At one point he suggested that writers should avoid the use of historical flashbacks to start episodes because the series had used a few of these close together, but they are now allowed once again. 'It was just so that viewers didn't think the same thing was happening as the previous week,' he says. 'Also the flashback works best when it is indicative of the process Barnaby's mind is going through.' For example, Barnaby may see something in part one of the programme that seems insignificant at the time. However, in part six a flashback to this scene may allow the viewer to think back along with Barnaby and realize its importance. Another important use of the flashback is to enable viewers to actually see murders being committed.

There is also a positive move towards the development of the regular characters. Troy, for example, has changed considerably from his earliest incarnation in 'The Killings at Badger's Drift' and the relationship between him and Barnaby is always maturing. 'We may, for instance, try to find a source of mild contention between them, a temporary wedge,' Christopher reveals, explaining that, through such little spats, we may, at times, learn more about the personalities of the characters. But the relationship between Barnaby and Troy is unlikely to change radically. 'We have never set out to copy *Inspector Morse*,' says Betty Willingale, 'but like Morse's Lewis, Troy will stay as a sergeant for years. The strength of the series would be lost if we broke up the relationship with Barnaby.'

The character of Joyce Barnaby may seem insignificant in some respects but, according to Christopher, she is 'hugely important' because she allows Tom Barnaby to discuss the case at home. He is keen to keep in more of these domestic scenes, which are often cut because of over-runs. 'I like to leave a decent amount of material for the editor to work with, so that you're squeezing a quart into a pint pot rather than padding out an episode. But I intend to cut things back in future so that there is less over-run and we can see more of the Barnabys at home.'

Once a script has been finalized and the film shot, the powers that be at ITV need to be satisfied that its content won't offend the viewer. A compliance licensee is brought in to provide this guarantee but sometimes this officer's views do not coincide with those of the production team and, in particular, the script writer. Right from the start, *Midsomer Murders* ran into conflict with compliance when one scene involving incest had to be cut. 'We were negotiating about how many frames to cut out and how many pants and puffs we could keep in, this sort of thing,' explains Brian True-May. There was also an objection to a scene where Troy refused permission for an undertaker to take away a body, only for the undertaker to

'We have never set out to copy Inspector Morse but like Morse's Lewis, Troy will stay as a sergeant for years. The strength of the series would be lost if we broke up the relationship with Barnaby.'

remark to Barnaby: 'You have a right constable there.' The innuendo ruffled a few feathers, but Bentley refused to change the line.

Writers have generally learned not to be too precious about their written words, knowing full well that edits are inevitable during the production process, but sometimes there is a cut too far. 'The only cut I ever had that really, really angered and upset me was in "Death's Shadow",' says Anthony Horowitz. 'That's my favourite episode. I've always loved that one because it's nutty and yet a profoundly solid story. Twenty-four hours before it was transmitted, however, somebody in compliance noticed a scene where a child is hanged in a ritual and simply snipped it out. It was done with a pair of scissors, so that some of the music track jumped: it was horrible. And nobody bothered to tell me, so I watched it being transmitted. That really hurt. It was just so disrespectful of not just me but everybody, including the audience. We had filmed it very, very delicately, of course. Jeremy Silberston, the director, was very careful.'

Brian True-May agrees that the compliance officer should be sympathetic to the creator's wishes. 'They need to understand drama and that certain things need to be kept in, that there's a reason for them', he says. Occasionally, however, something slips through that eludes both production team and compliance officer. One celebrity, it transpires, sued for defamation when she was mentioned in the script as not turning up for a social function. 'It was unfortunate, an accident', admits Brian, 'and it cost us £12,000. There was one transmission in the UK using her name, but then we had to re-record all the copies worldwide. That cost us a fortune.'

''Death's Shadow' is my favourite episode ... it's nutty and yet a profoundly solid story.'

It proves that the choice of names for characters is always a tricky issue. To forestall such problems, the compliance officer is supplied in advance with details of the names Bentley plans to use and checks to ensure there are no conflicts with real people. 'If, for example, we have a doctor in a programme then we need to check that there is no practising GP with the same name,' explains Christopher Penfold. It also explains why there are often so many far out names in *Midsomer Murders* – names that seem to stretch the writers' imagination almost as far as the plots.

While murders in Midsomer continue apace, there is little pressure for the series to develop much from its original concept. 'We only make five episodes a year, so we can't tie down large casts of actors,' explains producer Betty Willingale. 'We have a tight nucleus of running characters and it's not like a soap opera, where you have to move on. Anyway, it's been a big success, so why change the format in any way?'

From Page to Screen

Turning the written page into a television spectacle is not as easy as it may seem. 'They're very different animals,' explains Anthony Horowitz, who adapted two of the books: *The Killings at Badger's Drift* and *Written in Blood*. 'Books work in totally different ways. With a film you're stuck with five commercial breaks, requiring five climaxes. You obviously have a limited budget and you can have only a certain number of characters before the audience gets confused.' But Anthony did find plenty to work with in Caroline Graham's texts.

'I was enormously impressed by the books. Unlike many crime novels, they actually work. If you take some books and start to deconstruct them, you realize there are holes in them the size of the Grand Canyon that, as a dramatist, you have to fill. Caroline's books did not have that. *Written in Blood* was my favourite. I pressed very hard for that to be the first episode but Betty Willingale, very wisely, said no and we did *Badger's Drift* as the pilot.' Anthony's adaptation of this novel proved to be quite true to the original. 'I had to compress a certain amount because there was too much in the book, but by and large I did stick pretty closely to it.' Anthony was particularly pleased by the opening sequence, where an old lady discovers a couple making love in the open air. 'It set the whole tone of the series,' he says. 'Here you have sex in a wood, so it's modern, and yet the old lady on her tricycle seems to come from the 1930s.' The sequence also beautifully exposed the inspiration behind *Midsomer Murders* – the traditional whodunnit. 'There's a creaking gate, a hand reaching for the door: classic Agatha Christie,' he says.

The next film caused a few more problems, however. '"Written in Blood" is the only script I wrote where I had to tear it up and start again,' Anthony admits. 'Having loved it as a book, it became very, very difficult to adapt. In fact we created a whole second murder in that episode. That was really taking liberties. When you adapt Agatha Christie, the rule is the murderer, the person who's killed and the method of murder can never be changed: you can't add murders. But I felt very strongly that "Written in Blood" needed a second murder to keep it moving. If the writer figure had been kept alive, he'd have been able to explain everything and that would have left Barnaby with nothing to do. That's why I had to kill him.'

Anthony considered an interesting twist for the finale. 'I was very interested in Sue Clapper, the wife of the drama teacher, as a character,' he says. 'In my first draft, she was writing a murder mystery and the film finished, as I wrote it, with her selling what was basically the novel *Written in Blood* – she writes the whole novel, based on what had happened in her village. It was a lovely idea but it just didn't work. Betty, a brilliant script editor, the best in the business, knew it was wrong and showed me why. So we had to start again.'

For Anthony, the role of the adapter is, first of all, to be invisible. 'A good adaptation doesn't feel like an adaptation at all', he says. 'It feels as if the book has just somehow become a TV show.' Technically, the process begins with a close analysis of the written work. 'You read the book once for pleasure and then you read it a second time with a pen and start pulling out what you can and can't use. In "Written in Blood", for instance, we cut down the number of stories that were going on. There were just too many.' The process of completing a script then takes Anthony about two months – 'a month for the first draft and then another month for the polishes', he reveals. 'I'm a fast writer, though. The biggest challenge is how to make the format fresh and interesting, so it doesn't feel the same as every other murder mystery you've ever seen. With *Midsomer Murders* that was easy because we had such eccentric characters to play with, and all the sub-stories – the red herrings – were in themselves wonderfully rich.'

Excerpts from the script for 'Judgement Day'.

If the audience pinpoints the murderer too early, Anthony is not duly worried. 'By and large people don't guess mine. Obviously, some people will, but I have a number of people I test my stories out on. But, to my mind, a good murder mystery has this quality that, when you come to the end, you get the "Oh of course it was" feeling: you're not totally surprised. "Of course, it makes sense: I should have seen that" – that's the reaction you're aiming for. So if the killer is completely and utterly unknown, for some reason, you've not satisfied the audience. If an audience member guesses it, that doesn't mean you've failed. On the contrary, the pleasure of guessing who did it, if it's clever enough, is as good as not guessing it.'

'Writing a murder mystery is not like performing a magic trick. You're not out to deceive people or fool people: you're out to beguile them.'

TROY
We'll do what we can, sir.

As ever, BARNABY picks up what TROY has missed.

BARNABY
If you don't mind my asking, sir, how do you know there were two of them?

EDWARD
I'm sorry?

BARNABY
You said "little bastards". Plural. It could have been just one.

EDWARD
(Thrown) Well...I assumed. They always come in pairs, don't they?

CUT TO

32.   EXT. GREYFRIARS HOUSE DAY.

BARNABY and TROY walk down to the gate where the tyre marks gouged into the gravel by the van can be clearly seen.

TROY
You don't think he was lying, do you? About being out of the house?

A shrug from BARNABY. He looks down at the tyre marks.

TROY
Those were made last night. I've checked them. They don't match his car. They could belong to the white van.

BARNABY
Quite possibly, Troy. But these tyre tracks are quite clearly turning that way. (Points) But surely the London road is over there...

TROY
So if Allardice was coming from London...

Midsomer Murders Writers

Anthony Horowitz

'The Killings at Badger's Drift'; 'Written in Blood'; 'Death's Shadow'; 'Strangler's Wood'; 'Dead Man's Eleven'; 'Judgement Day'

As first writer, Anthony Horowitz laid down the framework and set the standard for other writers wishing to take on the daunting task of scripting a *Midsomer Murders* episode. His other major writing credits include many episodes of *Agatha Christie's Poirot*, *Robin of Sherwood*, *The Saint*, *William Tell*, *Anna Lee*, *Murder Most Horrid*, *Murder in Mind* and his own creations, *Crime Traveller* and *Foyle's War*. He is also a successful writer of children's books.

Caroline Graham

'Death of a Hollow Man'

Barnaby's creator, Caroline Graham, adapted one of her own novels for series one. This followed work on episodes of *Crossroads*.

Douglas Watkinson

'Faithful Unto Death'; 'Death in Disguise'; 'Blood Will Out'; 'Beyond the Grave'; 'Death of a Stranger'

Douglas Watkinson's work has taken in both drama and comedy, the former illustrated by episodes of *The Onedin Line*, *The Professionals*, *Maybury*, *Juliet Bravo*, *Boon*, *Emmerdale* and *Poirot*; the latter by his own sitcoms *The New Statesman* (a BBC production, not to be confused with Rik Mayall's later ITV hit) and *Sweet Sixteen*.

Hugh Whitemore

'Blue Herrings'

A major source of quality single dramas, Hugh Whitemore has been writing for television since the 1960s. His best-known contributions have included *The Adventures of Don Quixote*, *84 Charing Cross Road* and *Dummy*, interspersed with work on major series such as *Elizabeth R*, *Cider with Rosie*, *Rebecca*, *I Remember Nelson*, *The Rector's Wife*, *Breaking the Code* and *A Dance to the Music of Time*.

Christopher Russell

'Garden of Death'; 'Ring Out Your Dead'
Episodes of *Bergerac*, *The Bill*, *Cadfael* and *An Unsuitable Job for a Woman*
number among Christopher Russell's notable writing credits.

David Hoskins

'Destroying Angel'; 'Tainted Fruit'
Although his background is in comedy writing, David Hoskins was also one of the key writers on *The Bill* for a number of years.

Terry Hodgkinson

'The Electric Vendetta'
Terry Hodgkinson's television work has included episodes of *Wish Me Luck* and *Ballykissangel*.

Jeremy Paul

'Who Killed Cock Robin?'
With scripts for series as notable as *Upstairs, Downstairs*, *Country Matters*, *The Adventures of Sherlock Holmes* and *Hetty Wainthropp Investigates*, Jeremy Paul's writing pedigree speaks for itself. Jeremy also co-wrote (with Alan Gibson) the futuristic *Play for Today* dramas 'The Flipside of Dominick Hide' and 'Another Flip for Dominick'.

                    TROY
        Go on.

                    RAY
        Maybe you could talk to Peter
        Drinkwater.

In the background, JACK stops working.

                    RAY
        He's Mary Drinkwater's nephew. Her
        great nephew. He come back at the start
        of the year. Lived with her for a while but
        then he moved into the old farm.
        Windywhistle Farm. It's deserted now.

                    TROY
        Peter Drinkwater.

                    RAY
        He's a young lad. A bit on the wild side.
        Not that I'm saying he'd get himself in
        any trouble, mind. But you asked!

                                    CUT TO

34.   EXT. RAY DORSET'S SHOP   DAY.

BARNABY and TROY leave.

                    BARNABY
        Peter Drinkwater. I have a feeling that
        name rings a bell.

                    TROY
        Do you want to see him?

                    BARNABY
        Unless you have other plans…

They get into the car.

                                    CUT TO

Peter J Hammond

'Dark Autumn'
P J Hammond is a vastly experienced television writer, well known for work on series such as *Dixon of Dock Green*, *The Sweeney*, *The Bill*, *Hazell*, *Hunter's Walk*, *Ace of Wands*, *Perfect Scoundrels*, *EastEnders*, *Emmerdale*, *Doctor Finlay* and *Dangerfield*. In the 1970s he was script editor for *Z Cars* and created the science fiction classic *Sapphire and Steel*. Hammond has also dabbled in comedy, devising and writing the 1980s' sitcom *Lame Ducks*.

Andrew Payne

'Murder on St Malley's Day'; 'Market for Murder'
Andrew Payne is probably best known as creator of the gourmet detective series *Pie in the Sky*. His other work has included scripts for *Minder* and *Shoestring*.

Michael Russell

'A Worm in the Bud'
Michael Russell has lent his writing talents to numerous popular TV dramas. These have included *Emmerdale*, *All Creatures Great and Small*, *Between the Lines*, *Heartbeat* and *The Tales of Para Handy*.

---

35.   INT. RAY DORSET'S SHOP   DAY.

RAY watches BARNABY and TROY leave, at the same time slicing meat. JACK comes forward.

> JACK
> Why did you have to do that? Why did you have to talk about Peter that way?

> RAY
> I could have said more than I did.

> JACK
> He's my friend, dad!

> RAY
> He's trouble. He's leading you into trouble and I wish he'd never come here. Sometimes I want to…

> JACK
> What?

> RAY
> Nothing. Never you mind.

RAY is still holding the butcher's knife. He slices open a joint of meat.

                                                    CUT TO

36.   INT. LAURA'S BEDROOM   DAY.

An almost exact replay of Scene 30. PETER DRINKWATER, half-naked, with the gold chain in place, rolls onto his back. But this time the image is a even seedier. He's in bed with LAURA BRIERLY - with an age gap of about twenty years she's very much the older woman. Worse, this is her bedroom (Habitat with country chintz) and her marital bed.

> LAURA
> What time is it?

> PETER
> Twelve.

> LAURA
> Gordon will be back soon. It's his afternoon surgery. You have to go.

Midsomer Mood Music

There's almost as much mystery in the music of *Midsomer Murders* as in solving the crimes. Consider the distinctive, electronic swirl that characterizes the programme's theme tune and other incidental music: a peculiar, tuneful wail that is generated by a remarkable instrument – one that is played without even being touched.

The man behind the eerie title theme and all the 'mood' music underscoring each episode is Jim Parker, a four-time BAFTA award winner and veteran of such TV hits as *Soldier, Soldier*, *House of Cards*, *Moll Flanders*, *Tom Jones* and *A Rather English Marriage*. Jim was invited to write the score for the pilot episode, 'The Killings at Badger's Drift', by producer Betty Willingale and director Jeremy Silberston, with whom he had worked on *The House of Eliott*. 'They briefed me on what it was about and who was going to be in it and my first job was to come up with a good theme tune,' Jim remembers. 'I put down various themes on my keyboard and played them back to Betty and Jeremy. Fortunately, one piece jumped out at Jeremy straight away.'

There are between 35 and 50 different pieces of music, of varying lengths, in each episode

Still known simply as 'Midsomer Murders' that quirky tune is re-recorded fresh for every episode, to fit the length of track required and to set the mood of each individual production. What lifts it above the ordinary is that melodic electronic wail, which comes from a bizarre instrument called a theremin. This was invented in Russia in 1919 by physicist Leon Theremin, who had noticed the strange screeching noise given off by the valve radios of the time if someone stood too close to them. Studying this, he devised an early form of synthesiser, but one that is never touched by the player. The right hand moves around an antenna to control the pitch and the left adjusts the volume in the same way.

Jim brings in acknowledged theremin specialist Celia Sheen to play the instrument and her contribution is added after a small orchestra of strings, horns and keyboards has laid down the core of each piece of music for the episode. The musicians are all top London players and are described by Jim as 'the crème de la crème'. They perform an accompaniment to the final edited film and the music is then digitally locked onto the production. This comes, of course, after Jim has prepared the entire score.

[the] melodic electronic wail ... comes from a bizarre instrument called a theremin

'I see the script and I also attend the read-through', he explains, 'but I don't do any more until I see the final edited film – unless there's a song or specific piece of music needed in advance – because you don't know how much music is going to be required. I watch the film with the producer and director and we agree where music needs to be added and what sort.' Jim then has about a month to write and record the music but after about 10 days he usually has the basic score in place. 'I record it on my keyboard at home and play it back along with the film to the production team. If it's all agreed then I orchestrate the score for the musicians and we set about recording the final version, using real cellos and violins instead of my synthesiser.'

An ear for Murder: BAFTA award-winner Jim Parker.

There are between 35 and 50 different pieces of music, of varying lengths, in each episode, a legacy of the success of the pilot episode. '"Badger's Drift" seemed to need a lot of music, so the style was set for the series and we've stuck to it,' explains Jim. 'The aim is to add to the film but not duplicate what it is saying. Clues, for instance, tend to be reasonably obvious, so there's no need to underline them with music, but we can use music to set false moods. Take a car driving along a road: music can give the impression that the driver is up to no good.'

With so many red herrings like this littering each episode, it is all too easy to underestimate the importance of Jim's mysterious music.

Making Murder Look Easy

If there's one man Chief Inspector Barnaby ought to put behind bars it is Colin Skeaping. He's the man responsible for most of the murders in Midsomer. As stunt co-ordinator, it is his job to dream up the most fantastic ways of disposing of people, and yet make everything look absolutely real.

A stuntman or stunt co-ordinator for 35 years, Colin has worked with most of the big names in the movie business but has turned to television in recent years in order to spend more time at home. After the white-knuckle action of several Bond and Disney films, and doubling for Luke Skywalker in the first three *Star Wars* movies, the more sedate world of rural murder provides a graceful way of winding down. Colin joined Midsomer in the second series (replacing fellow stunt experts Dave Holland and Stuart St Paul), at the invitation of associate producer Ian Strachan with whom he'd worked in the past. The challenge, he says, is in tailoring the stunt to suit the mood of the programme. 'Although, on the surface of it, *Midsomer Murders* does not appear to be a particularly "stunty" show, there's an awful lot of killing going on and we have to devise different and original ways of killing people and make it look effective. We've had quite a few fights, one or two car stunts, some high falls, somebody falling from rafters on to some farm machinery, and it all has to be done within the atmosphere and framework of *Midsomer Murders*.'

The Midsomer Murder Rate

In the 23 episodes of Midsomer Murders *so far recorded there have been no less than 87 suspicious deaths, of which 68 have proved to be murders – an average of just under three murders per episode. There have been six suicides, five cases of death from natural causes and eight accidental deaths.*

Colin's work begins with the delivery of the script. 'I read the script, mark parts where I think my input would be required and then discuss those with the associate producer and possibly the director. Then we go and look at locations and talk about how we're going to shoot the stunts, discussing with the director what he would like to see and suggesting the best way to make it look real. It's then a question of rehearsing the actors, getting in the stunt doubles where required and making a sequence out of it.'

A day's work for Colin might be supervising someone falling from an 80ft tower, being stabbed by a pitchfork or crashing into a combine harvester. 'The combine harvester stunt was fun to do,' he recalls. 'We had to make up a dummy front for the harvester that my stunt driver could realistically crash into, because obviously combine harvesters are expensive. We mounted this "crashable" section onto the back of a large lorry and the stuntman drove the car into that. Then we cut to see the stuntman coming out through the windscreen.' The technique, he explains, is to break the action down into parts, film it and then put it all together. To shatter the windscreen, detonators are placed on the corners. Today's laminated glass, however, makes the job more difficult. 'All cars used to be fitted with toughened glass which shattered when you fired the

All in a day's work: Barnaby and Bullard survey the stuntman's handiwork.

All of a quiver: Barnaby inspects yet another victim in 'Death's Shadow'.

Opposite: The crew close in on a particularly shocking murder in 'Tainted Fruit'.

detonators,' Colin explains. 'Laminated glass spider-webs and doesn't come out'. It is just one of the problems facing today's stunt arranger. 'All the safety aids that have been incorporated into cars over the last 15 years have worked against us. As a stuntman, you don't want any safety aids – anti-lock brakes, traction control, laminated glass, air bags – all these things have to be disabled if you want to do a decent stunt sequence.'

Making sure the stunt works first time is often of paramount importance. 'If you are smashing something up, or you need a lot of time to re-set what you are doing, then obviously you don't want to have to do it twice,' Colin reveals. 'To make sure, you rehearse everything up to the point of the stunt as well as you possibly can, you remove all variables and you discourage directors from shooting a long sequence with a stunt at the end of it. This is just in case something earlier in the take has made it unusable. For example, you don't want to have a big car crash in the same shot as you've had a lot of dialogue, in case the dialogue has not worked and you've got to re-shoot the whole thing. You try to organize it so that the stunt is done in isolation. If you're turning a car over, it's a one off. The car won't be usable again in the time available and preparing another one would be out of the question.'

A character leaping from a tower is less of a challenge, it seems. 'For falls over about 40ft we generally use air bags,' Colin says, referring to the soft landing awaiting the faller. 'They're more comfortable than boxes, which are a bit old-fashioned.' He insists on using real people to take the tumble because dummies, even articulated ones, don't look real when they fall. 'The heads and knees go the wrong way and you don't get the appearance of a human being. Any shot using a dummy has to be very, very quick. If you want to hold on somebody somersaulting through the air, it's got to be a real person.' The process is simple. The actor begins the leap from the top of the tower but lands on a crash mat on a scaffolding platform just a few feet down. The action is cut and later a stunt double performs the leap for real, but shot at a distance so his identity is vague. He lands on the air bag. The actor then replaces him for the close up shots on the ground. The sequence in which all this is shot may vary, but with skilful editing together, it can look extremely effective.

A character leaping from a tower is less of a challenge

One famous scene involved the death of a man in a burning caravan – again not a difficult effect to achieve according to the modest Mr Skeaping. 'We used a controlled fire effect while he was in the caravan, using what are called flame bars – bars with a gas feed and little holes that you light. You turn them up to whatever height you want between the actor and the camera, or have them staged around the set, to make it appear as if the whole place is burning. Then,

when you want to see the whole thing going up in flames, of course, you take the actor out. For effect, you might do a tight shot on his face at the window with flames appearing to be round him.'

In another episode, a man is found hanged in the woods. 'The technique is that you put somebody in a full harness with a wire going up through the rope. Then you put a loose bit of rope, which isn't attached to anything, around the neck and let the head flop to one side to appear that they've been hanged.' It's easy when you know how, but clearly not something to try at home.

The use of doubles is an important part of the stunt game, but *Midsomer Murders* doesn't employ regular look-alikes for its main stars. 'We haven't had any one person to double John or Daniel all the way through,' Colin explains, 'because television engagements are always fairly

short – one or two days, scattered about. You have to see who's available at the time. Also it depends on what type of stunt is involved. If it's a car stunt then I'll obviously look at people who are good drivers; if it's a fall from the rafters then I'll look at somebody who is good at high falls.'

A large part of Colin's job involves supervising actors doing their own action shots. 'John Nettles is a very good person to work with,' he says, 'because he's happy to rely on the stunt co-ordinator to advise him on what is safe for him to do and what isn't. If a stuntman gets hurt, I can get another one the next day, but if the star gets hurt then we've got a problem.'

> 'If a stuntman gets hurt, I can get another one the next day, but if the star gets hurt then we've got a problem.'

But another day means another challenge for Colin. 'Invention comes into it every time', he says. 'That's what's so nice about the work. No two jobs are ever the same. Yes, you rely on your experience – where you have done stunts of a similar nature – but you always adapt to suit your present circumstances.'

From the matter-of-fact way in which he describes his work you can't help drawing comparisons with the cold, calculating killers who stalk the village lanes of Midsomer. In fact, the truth is out: by his own admission, most of the murders have indeed been committed by Colin himself. 'Generally, if there's a pair of hands behind a weapon and you don't see anybody else, and don't need to see who does the killing,' he says, 'it'll be me.'

Bizarre Murder Implements

Knives, shotguns and poison are all par for the course, but here are some of Midsomer's most inventive murder weapons:

Ashtray	Drinks cabinet	Slide projector
Billhook	Electricity	Spade
Bow and arrow	Liquid nicotine	Switch blade razor
Candlestick	Ornamental sword	Syringe
Cricket bat	Pillow	Walking stick
Desk	Pitchfork	Wrench
Doped horse	Plough	

The Real Midsomer

The appeal of *Midsomer Murders* is multi-dimensional. There's the classic whodunnit, of course, plus the roll-call of hugely talented guest stars and regular performers. Then there are the magnificent settings. For the Englishman abroad, an episode of *Midsomer Murders* acts almost as a postcard from home. Quaint villages, where the sun nearly always shines, may not be a strictly truthful expression of British life in the 21st century, but they are certainly more likely to induce a bout of homesickness than a vision of the M25 motorway on a wet Friday night. For the anglophile, the homely pub, the village green and a row of thatched cottages are without question better symbols of beautiful Britain than graffiti-stained concrete car parks or inner-city squalor.

Midsomer Murders is filmed mostly in the counties of Buckinghamshire and Oxfordshire, with occasional excursions into Berkshire and Hertfordshire. In Caroline Graham's books, the town of Causton, with its ring of blood-splattered villages, is positioned somewhere north of Slough, close to Uxbridge and Gerrard's Cross. For television, the action has been re-located further west. The Thames-side town of Wallingford doubles for Causton and the town's Corn Exchange has featured strongly as the Causton Corn Exchange, home of the Causton Players amateur dramatics society. Some smaller settlements fringing Wallingford, including Ewelme, Brightwell Baldwin and Watlington, have also

Holy Trinity Church, Bledlow, Bucks, a.k.a. St Michael's at Badger's Drift.

played their parts but other locations are scattered over a wider area in and around the Chiltern hills, bounded roughly by Aylesbury in the north, Reading in the south, Oxford in the west and the M25 in the east.

The job of finding all these stunning, evocative venues has fallen mostly to location manager Georgina Hamilton. Georgina, daughter of producer Brian True-May, also worked on *The Ruth Rendell Mysteries* and has lived in the Chilterns area for years. It was once fancifully reported that Georgina researches all the locations on horseback, but the truth is more mundane and petrol-driven. Her many motorised forays into deepest 'Midsomer' have left such a deep impression on her photographic memory that she can usually pinpoint a likely location as

The Thames-side town of Wallingford doubles for Causton

soon as she has read a script. 'I keep a good map and mark on it places I think may be useful in the future,' she reveals. 'If I happen to drive past a lovely, ramshackle old cottage, I tend to make a note of it. I may even stop and speak to the owner there and then, to see if they'd be interested in our using it. That saves time later. When a script arrives, I write down a list of the locations required. I usually have plenty of places in mind and then take the director and the designer to visit them to see what they think.'

'The director needs to see how the location can be used to develop the characters and also how the filming can work. Some have a clear-cut picture of what they need but others have to be shown what is available. Sometimes the location I've suggested clicks first time; at other times we need to look at a few more possibilities.'

The Lions at Bledlow: a Midsomer local on more than one occasion.

Finding the right location is not just a matter of spotting the right house. For a start a building that looks perfect from the outside may not be suitable at all internally. 'We don't have the huge budget of a feature film, so the locations have to be more or less right: we can't afford to change things very much,' Georgina explains. 'If we can, we try not to use the exterior of one building and then the inside of another for the same place. That just adds to the time and trouble. But sometimes we do have a problem with little cottages. They need to look small outside but then there's not enough room inside.'

Director Jeremy Silberston underlines how this can be a headache. 'When it comes to

shooting interiors, you've got to think about how you can get in all the equipment and people, including the crew behind the camera,' he says. 'I remember we used a very, very small police interview room in early episodes and that was a squeeze.' There's also a question of safety. 'You've also got to consider whether a tower, for instance – as in "Death's Shadow" – can physically support the team and the equipment.'

Sometimes, however, the right location just cannot be found, so a little improvization is called for. The house owned by Iris and Dennis Rainbird in 'The Killings at Badger's Drift' was one such challenge. 'We found a house in Little Missenden that had an interesting quality to which we could add an observation post,' Jeremy reveals, 'but, when it came to close ups, we used a mock up in a field around the corner, only 3–4ft above the ground, so the actors didn't need to go climbing over roofs.'

Very often the whole village set-up has to be fabricated to fit the story line. 'Villages never work out the way that writers have planned,' says Brian True-May. 'The script might call for the church to be here, the village hall there, someone's house there, so we might use three villages just to make up one. Barnaby and Troy might get out of their car, turn around the corner and then we cut to a completely different village, but you wouldn't know. It's the only way to get the geography to work.' But there is an added complication as far as the setting for *Midsomer Murders* is concerned in that due care is needed when mixing and matching different

Above: The Lee, Bucks, better known as Badger's Drift.

Overleaf: The real and the fictional Midsomers.

> '*The script might call for the church to be here, the village hall there, someone's house there, so we might use three villages just to make up one.*'

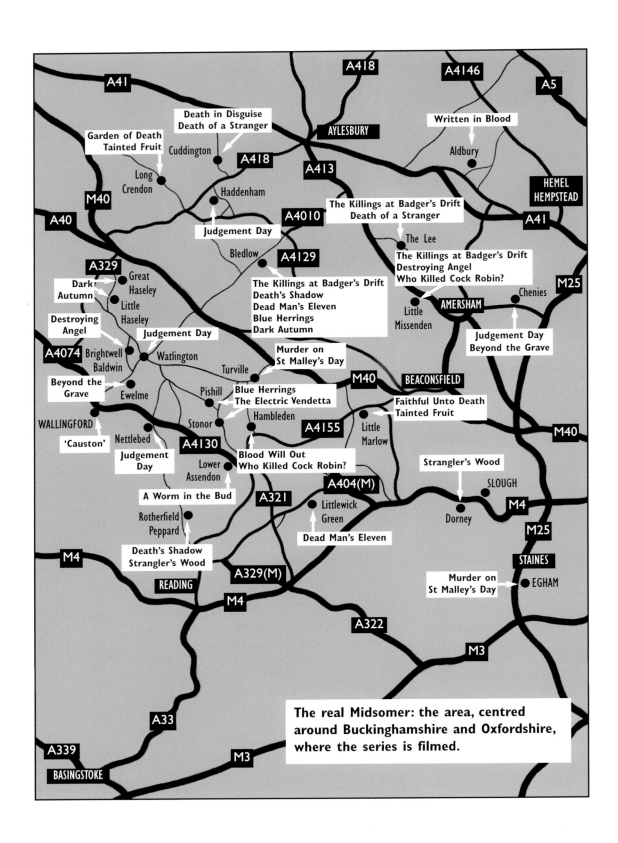

The real Midsomer: the area, centred around Buckinghamshire and Oxfordshire, where the series is filmed.

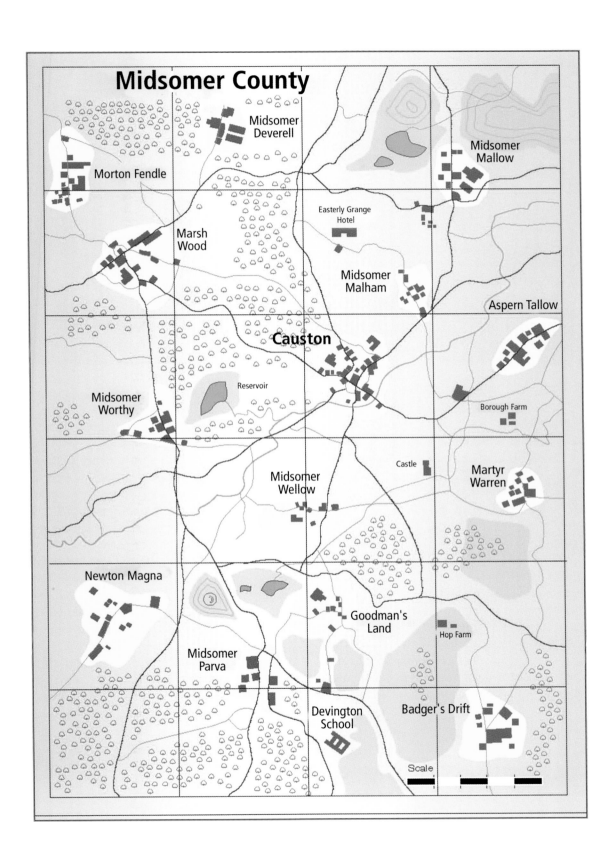

Downtown Causton: Wallingford and its Corn Exchange.

villages. 'We have flint and brick in the Chilterns and when you move a bit further towards Oxford it suddenly becomes stone and thatch,' explains Brian.

Locations also need to have enough space to accommodate the support team, including parking for make-up, wardrobe and catering vans, and then there's the matter of noise. 'In early episodes we used a police station in Gerrard's Cross, but that was near a road,' says Georgina. 'Also, we had to schedule our filming to fit in with police rotas, so in the end we built a special set on a campus in Bushey.'

A major part of Georgina's work is arranging the filming with the residents. 'I think it helps being a woman,' she says. 'Some people can be put off and worried if the initial approach is wrong. But most people like the idea. The big mansions and manor houses seem to need the money and other people find it exciting to have their house in the programme. It's only really rich people, who don't need the money, who aren't interested.'

> **Before filming begins much effort goes into ensuring the inhabitants of a village are all on board**

Before filming begins much effort goes into ensuring the inhabitants of a village are all on board. 'We send out leaflets and have meetings with the parish council and the church,' says Georgina. 'We knock on doors and talk to as many people as we can, so that everyone is aware of what we're doing. We make sure we get all the right permissions and make donations to the village. We also tend to use village halls for things like car parking, so we're putting money back into the village in this way, too.'

One of the reasons for involving the whole village in the production is to help prevent potentially disruptive local activities, such as hedge cutting or lawn mowing. 'Even the noise of one lawn mower can ruin filming,' says Georgina. 'But we do make every effort to let everyone know well in advance to avoid these problems'. Occasionally, however, diplomacy and a cash reward fail to make a difference and one or two individuals, who, for some reason, feel hard done by, do their best to obstruct the work of the crew, by denying permission to lay camera tracks in front of their house or some other frustrating act.

Filming in the town is surprisingly not problematical. The people of Wallingford are very co-operative, according to Brian True-May. 'We just carry on. We get help from the police if we need to stop traffic but, if we're doing a broad shot, we let everything carry on and do it in the middle. It's not like filming in the middle of London, which is almost impossible. Wallingford people are very friendly and they like the exposure, although we've been asked not to do any more with the theatre'.

Some places have now decided to call time on film work. Aldbury, near Tring in Hertfordshire – the setting for 'Written in Blood' – is one such location, Brian reveals. 'It's been used so many times for films that the residents are just fed up. Recently somebody suggested shooting at Aldbury, but I said no. Hambleden ('Blood Will Out' and 'Who Killed Cock Robin?') is another one. They just get too much filming and become very recognizable.'

However, after 23 episodes, the biggest problem facing the team is finding brand new locations, which means old locations being re-shot from different angles. Brian is looking to turn this to the series' advantage. 'I've encouraged the writers to bring in some of the same villages again and call them the same names,' he says, accepting that it's all fiction anyway. 'We all know it's impossible for all these murders to take place, so why not have a few more in the same village a few years later.'

Above: View over Ewelme – Aspern Tallow in 'Beyond the Grave'.

Left: The Queen's Head at Little Marlow, well-frequented in 'Faithful Unto Death'.

At work in Wallingford.

The Changing Face of Causton

Causton, as we see it, is a modest little rural town, served by trains from London Marylebone. Not much is revealed about the town itself, except that it has a prominent comprehensive school (Troy's alma mater), the Causton Institute for evening classes, and a hospital. The main feature in the centre of town is the Corn Exchange (a.k.a. the Causton Playhouse), home of the Causton Players, which sits next to a branch of Lloyds Bank. Other entertainment is provided by The Roxy cinema. The town also has a branch of the Midsomer Building Society and among the shops is a bookstore called The Blackbird. Professional services are provided by Jocelyne, Tibbles and Delaney solicitors and Ericson's estate agents.

The Causton depicted by Caroline Graham in her novels is slightly better defined than the TV Causton. Graham places the town 12 miles from Slough along the B416. The municipality is run by Causton Borough Council and amenities on hand include Causton Tech, a cattle market and branches of the Nat West bank and Coalport and National Building Society. Causton Amateur Dramatic Society (CADS) performs at the Latimer Theatre, on the corner of the main street, with, no doubt, members of the Causton Arts Circle in the audience and first night reports in the *Causton Echo* or the *South-East Bucks Observer*. There is no Sainsbury's or Marks & Spencer, but the town does have a Gateway supermarket and its own department store, Bobby's. Other shopping opportunities are supplied by The Blackbird bookshop and The Spinning Wheel antiques emporium (although this is also listed as The Magpie on one occasion). To eat, there's a choice of the Soft Shoe Café and the more upmarket Bunter's tea rooms. For further relaxation, Caustonians can fall back on the Jolly Cavalier pub or the Golden Fleece Hotel. The latter, regrettably, has a reputation for sordid activities, though is perhaps not as seedy as the backstreet Casa Nova Club. When the excitement becomes too much to bear, undertakers Rainbird and Gillis see to every last request.

The Midsomer Pub Guide

A pint of real ale in a cosy, beamed pub is part of the attraction of life in lovely Midsomer. Not surprisingly, therefore, most villages featured in the series have their own pub. Some are not named; some are named but never seen; in some cases pubs are seen but not referred to and are actually the pubs which serve the real-life villages where the episode was shot. One pub used more than once for filming is The Lions of Bledlow, at Bledlow, which featured as The Queen's Arms in 'Dead Man's Eleven', the pub in 'Blue Herrings' and The Sword & Sceptre in 'Dark Autumn'. From the information available in the series, a guide to Midsomer pubs would look like this.

Causton:	*The Deverell Arms Hotel*
	The Feathers Hotel
	(outside Causton on the London road)
Fletcher's Cross:	*The Queen's Arms*
Goodman's Land:	*The Plough; The Sword & Sceptre*
Martyr Warren:	*The Stag & Huntsman*
Midsomer Magna:	*The Red Lion*
Midsomer Malham:	*The Horseshoes*
Midsomer Mallow:	*The Crooked Billet*
Midsomer Parva:	*The Chalk & Gown; The Black Horse*
Midsomer Worthy:	*The Golden Ball*
Morton Fendle:	*The Queen's Head*
Newton Magna:	*The White Swan*

John Nettles is
DCI Barnaby

John Nettles and Jim Bergerac – two names that a decade ago seemed interchangeable. Ten years of playing the lone wolf Jersey policeman with a chronic drink problem fused actor and character so tightly together that they seemed indivisible. In the public perception, John always wore a leather bomber jacket and spent his waking hours dashing around the coves and bays of the Channel Islands in a classic red Triumph. Now, however, although viewers still see John as a relentless and determined police officer, the name he answers to on screen (and often in the street) is not Jim but Tom.

'It hadn't crossed my mind to go back into television, but this seemed an opportunity too good to miss.'

They may both be law enforcers, and their surnames may begin with the same letter, but that's where the similarities between Bergerac and Barnaby end. For whereas Bergerac was dynamic, aggressive and somewhat reckless, Barnaby is thoughtful, calm and reassuring. This is the contrast that helped John take the bold step of accepting another TV police challenge at a time when he wasn't entirely certain he wanted to return to television at all.

'After *Bergerac* finished, I re-joined the Royal Shakespeare Company, where I'd been for a while in the 1970s,' he recalls. 'I felt I had unfinished business there. I did one season, two seasons in Stratford that somehow turned into five. Then in 1995 I was approached by Brian True-May, who was thinking of dramatizing the Inspector Barnaby novels. He thought I'd be suitable for the role and asked me to read the books. I thought they were pretty damn good.' However, things went quiet and John put Barnaby firmly to the back of his mind. 'I was busy and had a lot of offers, so I forgot entirely about the project until I was called by Brian a year later to say that it was a runner. I can't say I was a "whodunnit" fan at the time, and it hadn't crossed my mind to go back into

television, but this seemed an opportunity too good to miss. There was to be no expense spared in production and the whole thing would be great fun.'

For research into his character, John talked to Barnaby's creator. 'I met Caroline Graham for lunch – she's a delightful lady – and found out what she really wanted from the character. I liked her sense of humour and her view of detective fiction. It's a comedic take on the whodunnit, in the glorious English tradition of the detective story, stretching back to Conan Doyle and before. It is almost, but not quite, a send up.'

> *'To be ordinary on screen is really quite difficult.'*

What also appealed to John was the sheer 'ordinariness' of the leading figure. 'Barnaby is not a loner like Bergerac; he's not an opera-loving romantic like Morse or a heart-on-the-sleeve agonizer like Frost. He's a suburban Middle Englander, in the long blush of middle-age. He wears cardigans and three-piece suits, drives a sensible car and enjoys his happy home. There are hints in Caroline's books that he has been through a troubled past – drink, stress and so on – but that's all behind him.'

For John, this underplay is central to the success of the series. 'There's enough psychological quirkiness around Barnaby so there's no need to add to it. He doesn't get in the way of the story. It's "whodunnit?" that is important, not "who solved it?".' All the same, the lack of distinctive personal traits makes a character much more of a challenge for an actor than one with a clear-cut style and personality. 'You have to keep stopping yourself adding to the character,' John reveals. 'To be ordinary on screen is really quite difficult.'

A family man: Tom with wife Joyce and daughter Cully.

John also admires Barnaby's humanness. 'I appreciate the way he never denigrates the loss of life,' he says. This contrasts with the more flippant attitude expressed by Barnaby's sidekick, Sgt Troy. 'Oh, there's a lovely tension there,' exclaims John. 'Troy is nowhere near as unpleasant as he is in the novels but there's still a harshness in him. I see them as almost a father and son pairing, albeit with the son as a bit of a hooligan.' As viewers will know, Barnaby does have occasion to bring his apprentice into line, but this is mostly done with gentle sarcasm. 'We had to watch how we played the sarcasm,' John admits. 'We needed to keep it light, in keeping with Barnaby's general nature.'

John and his on-screen partner Daniel Casey have a sparky relationship. 'He's horribly talented,' John admits. 'He's also, of course, much younger, but we try to make light of the age

> *'I did Brutus and Leontes and nobody noticed. Now I get fan mail for Barnaby from all over the world.'*

difference. He's a smashing lad and we get on very well. He's got a wicked sense of humour.' The respect is mutual. 'We're quite similar in many ways, I think,' agrees Daniel. 'We both want to have an enjoyable working day. You can work really, really hard and be very serious about your work but still have a good laugh. The work's going to be of a high standard then because people aren't going to be tense.'

Daniel draws parallels between the relationships shared by Barnaby and Troy and himself and John. 'There's a significant gap between John and me in age and career. He's so experienced and has done everything, while I'm still at the beginning. So, like me, Troy doesn't pose a threat. They do needle each other from time to time, however, and Barnaby enjoys watching him fumble around in the dark. John and I, on the other hand, get on very well.'

John claims to have loosely based Barnaby on two real-life policemen he knows well. 'I've covered a lot of research into the police over the years,' he says, 'in fact people have been known to think I am a policeman. When I was doing *Bergerac* I happened to call the police out to the scene of a real accident and the officers started asking me for orders! What I've done for Barnaby is to imitate a policeman's take on life, making him slightly removed and an observer. I do happen to know a lot about police work but let's remember that *Midsomer Murders* is Detective Fiction, with a capital D and F. Liberties are taken. If we were working on *Prime Suspect*, or even *The Bill*, then I'd need to look more closely at police procedures.'

On a personal level, John shrugs off suggestions that he and Barnaby have much in common. 'Tom is suburban to a degree, which I am not, and much more organized. He is unflappable, unlike me, we have a different sense of humour and I don't wear three-piece suits. What we do have in common is a happy marriage and a lovely daughter, plus a liking for a Rover 75!'

> '*We had Ian Thompson in "Blood Will Out". He's another person I hate because he's so talented.*'

Barnaby's domestic life is clearly important to him, a fact that John feels could be brought out a little more strongly in the series. 'Filming always tends to overrun,' he explains, 'and it is usually the little domestic scenes, the grace-mats as I call them, that tend to get cut, because they don't normally affect the story line. Which is a shame.' He and his on-screen wife, Jane Wymark, are great friends and before *Midsomer Murders* they appeared together in a film called *All Men Are Mortal*, based on a novel by Simone de Beauvoir. 'It should have been subtitled "But Not Mortal Enough",' John laughs. 'It was one of the worst films of the decade. On a scale of 1 to 10 it wouldn't have registered. It had enormous pretension but was laughable to behold.'

The third prong of the happy Barnaby home is actress daughter Cully, a character John feels strongly about, played by Laura Howard. 'Cully wasn't included in some episodes and I think she was missed. Barnaby needs to refer to her. He loses emotional depth if she's not there. It's just like in Shakespeare where there are so many important father-daughter relationships. We needed her back so I put my foot down. I also objected to the growing relationship between Cully and Troy. In reality, it would not have happened. Tom would not have put up with Troy calling round his house at all hours – they are business associates.'

It sounds as if John is calling all the shots but he insists that *Midsomer Murders* is very much a team effort. 'It's a family affair,' he confirms. 'I feel that unless you're having fun there's not much point in doing something. I've been on shows where the atmosphere has been unpleasant, because of overbearing stars or demanding producers, and I won't have it. Everyone involved is respected and cared for and I want to know why if that's not the case. Everyone's input is hugely important. We meet before each episode and all throw in suggestions about what has worked or will work.' Others are quick to praise the importance of John himself to the series. 'John Nettles is an unsung hero,' says director

Jeremy Silberston. 'He delivers all the time. It's tough being the lead character in a series, to have to turn up every day, be sure of knowing your lines – it can be demanding. But he does it with grace and charm. He is always hugely appreciative and is very concerned about the quality of the series and the calibre of the cast.'

Indeed, the wonderful roll call of guesting actors adds another dimension for John. 'I think it was Roger Moore who once said "I'm only here to make others look good," and that's how I feel now,' he modestly explains. 'I open the door and in come my favourite performers. We have "proper" actors on *Midsomer Murders* and, right from the first episode, when we had people like Rosalie Crutchley and Elizabeth Spriggs fleshing out the parts, it's been wonderful to see.

Another sad day at the office for Barnaby.

There's a great fund of British character actors that we draw from, including lots of great ladies of a certain age for whom there aren't many parts on television these days. Much of the credit has to go to my former wife, Joyce Nettles, who has done a terrific job as casting director.'

John mentions a few favourite guests that have added sparkle to the show. 'The Richard Briers episode ("Death's Shadow") made me laugh. He was great fun, so keen and enthusiastic, doing his own stunts and running around like a little gazelle. There was also Gordon Gostelow, making everyone laugh. You can't be in a scene with him because he steals it, which is exactly as it should be. I love the episode called "Blue Herrings", because it was so beautifully acted by people who were not young but had a lovely take on mortality. I looked at Phyllis Calvert, thought about all the fantastic people she had worked with and wondered at the fact that here she was, talking to me.'

Setting a good example: Barnaby and his ambitious bag carrier.

'But quite my favourite actor of all time is Alan Howard and it was a thrill to have him on the series. I'd been telling Daniel all about this marvellous actor and when he turned up for the read-through we observed him so closely that, when it was our turn, we both starting acting just like him.'

John's own acting career began at Southampton University. Adopted at birth, he was raised in Cornwall and attended St Austell Grammar School. 'Borstal-on-Sea,' he jokes. 'It's not there any more but it turned out some excellent people.' He graduated in History and Philosophy, taking an interest in drama during his studies. 'We entered a competition and staged *Caligula* for it. Somehow a famous critic gave me an ecstatic review and part of the reward was a chance to take the show to London. While we were there an agent asked me if he could represent me. I remember thinking that he was obviously expecting me to become an actor, and it made me think that perhaps that was what I wanted to do.' John joined the Royal Court Theatre and then moved into television. 'My first TV appearance was in a crime drama series called *The Expert*, which starred Marius Goring,' he remembers. 'Then I appeared in *A Family at War*, which was enormously successful at the time but failed dismally when it was repeated a few years ago. I was in the second series but they didn't show that again. Everyone thought it was too glum. That was a shame because they had re-negotiated my contract for repeat fees and I was looking forward to a nice cheque!' John was pleased to welcome a former *Family at War* co-star to the set of *Midsomer Murders*. 'We had Ian Thompson in "Blood Will Out". He's another person I hate because he's so talented. Why he hasn't had his own series I'll never know.'

> *'I've been on shows where the atmosphere has been unpleasant, because of overbearing stars or demanding producers, and I won't have it.'*

Another hugely popular series that featured John was *The Liver Birds*, in which he played the part of Paul, Sandra's (Nerys Hughes) boyfriend. 'When they revived the series in the 1990s they asked me if I wanted to go back, but I felt its time had gone. The premise of the series was the fun single, young girls could have and now they were middle-aged women. It was sad to see in a way.'

John then moved away from television, apart from a few minor roles, and back into the theatre, joining the RSC for the first time. A few years later, *Bergerac* beckoned and he was off to Jersey to become the unorthodox young sergeant fronting investigations by the island's Bureau des Etrangers. Although the series ended in 1991 after 10 years, he re-assumed the identity of Jim Bergerac for a cameo appearance alongside Jasper Carrott and Robert Powell in *The Detectives* a few years later. By this time, John had reluctantly left Jersey, a place he had made his home, because of work commitments. 'As beautiful as it is, Jersey is not a place to live if you're an actor and need to be in the West End or with the RSC,' he explains. He now lives near Stratford-upon-Avon. Although there were other television credits in series such as *Boon*, and the start of a flourishing voice-over career on documentaries such as *Airport* and *The Tourist Trap*, it was the RSC that absorbed most of John's time before the arrival of Inspector Barnaby.

'I remember thinking, should I do it or not?' John recalls. 'Is it a good career move? Then I thought, sod it: what career? I can have a good time. The public doesn't give a toss whether I've done *King Lear* or not. I did Brutus and Leontes and nobody noticed. Now I get fan mail for Barnaby from all over the world.'

Profile: DCI Tom Barnaby

Tom Barnaby is Causton CID's finest detective and a thoroughly nice man to boot. He doesn't smoke, gamble or swear and he drinks only in moderation. He prefers a Ford Mondeo or a Rover 75 to a vintage Jaguar, and seldom lays a finger on even the most filthy villain. He is, to take advantage of an over-used description, an 'ordinary bloke'.

Tom is a family man, doting on his wife of some 25 years, Joyce, and daughter Cully, with whom he lives in suburban Causton, just about far enough away for comfort from the bizarre goings on that litter his working day. *Chez* Barnaby is number 8, but the street is never mentioned, until Tom and Joyce move and take up residence at 6 Parchmore Close (although the number is later given as 7). Their phone number is 58632. The only turmoil in this deeply middle-class home life comes when Tom finds himself allergic to Cully's cat, or loses the battle of the bulge and is handcuffed by wife and daughter to a restrictive diet. The only other relation we see is his Auntie Alice, a gentle old lady whom he protects and adores.

A spot of gardening, a hand lent here and there behind the scenes of the Causton Playhouse, a good supper now and again with a glass of wine – these are the extents of this man's indulgences, although, as he turns out to be an ace Aunt Sally player, it seems our Tom must have frequented the pub a fair few times in his youth. But the viewer hungry for personal information lives on scraps: a visual clue like the little round badge on the lapel that signifies he belongs to the local rotary club, for instance, for precious little else is ever revealed about the linchpin of *Midsomer Murders*. Barnaby is a different creature from the personality detectives who have filled our screens since the 1950s.

In the novel Written in Blood, *Caroline Graham allows one of her characters to describe Barnaby and Troy in animal terms: while Troy is appropriately a 'ferret', Barnaby is clearly a 'badger'. On television, the emblem of the Midsomer Constabulary is also a badger.*

What we do know about Barnaby is that he is totally dedicated to his work. When the phone rings during supper, we know full well that he's on his way out of the door before the main course, because duty calls. Thankfully Joyce understands.

He becomes so obsessed with each case that his nights are sometimes shattered by stressful dreams suggesting yet another dimension to his investigation. For Tom, the open and shut case is never an option. Why take things at face value when there's so much more to be scratched out from beneath the surface? His method is to win the trust of the guilty with his calm, paternal manner and deceptive intelligence. A listener, not a talker, he proves remarkably successful in encouraging suspects to divulge information.

In Civvy Street, Barnaby is quite a cheerful chap, but he never makes light of his work and is appalled by violence and injustice. Should his right-hand man, Sgt Troy, chance a little black humour, his mentor is quick to put him in his place with a hard stare or a simple, well-chosen retort. His sense of fairness and his human touch even earn him respect among the criminal fraternity. It is almost disappointing, therefore, when our hero decides to bend the rules now and again. Entering a property without a warrant or the owner's permission is probably his greatest sin, although one that has caught him out on occasion. But most shocking of all was the time when he pulled rank to acquire two tickets for a sell-out play at the Causton Playhouse. After that, the occasional sarcastic remark to Troy seems barely worth mentioning.

John loosely based Barnaby on two real-life policemen he knows well

The original Tom Barnaby – the one created by Caroline Graham in her novels – is a little more colourfully drawn, but not much. We know that he was born in 1941 (the novels pre-date their TV equivalents by up to 10 years), is 6ft 3in tall and has brown eyes (John Nettles is 5ft 11in and has blue). He left school in the early 1950s. He and Joyce have lived at 17 Arbury Crescent for more than 20 years. They were married on 12 September 1973 and 'their song' is 'The Air That I Breathe' by The Hollies. His parents are still alive. Tom is a keen amateur artist, a devoted gardener and, The Hollies apart, a fan of the popular classics. As Joyce is an even worse cook in the novels than she appears on television, he is forced to take tablets to quell his bubbling stomach. Indeed, he even takes up cooking for self-preservation and thoroughly enjoys the experience. In the books, Barnaby never needs more than six hours sleep a night. He once smoked 50 cigarettes a day but now, fully reformed, has joined the lobby for clean air. In his career, he's seen it all. He'd joined the force soon after leaving school and suffered many a humiliation as a green, young copper. Toughing up, he became as hard and as plain-speaking as the rest but a mid-life crisis saw him take a softer, more considered tone, earning respect – not demanding it – along the way, creating the strong but subtle Barnaby we know today.

Daniel Casey is Sergeant Troy

The reporter's face was a picture. 'What's it like working with John Nettles?', she'd asked. It seemed an innocuous question to put to Daniel Casey but the answer was not the one she expected. 'It's horrible. He's an awful man,' he announced. 'He puts on this nice front but he's actually not a very nice man at all.' Daniel still chuckles at his little prank. 'She didn't know what to make of it,' he says, until he revealed he was only joking. He actually describes the working relationship as 'fabulous'. 'We do have really good fun. He takes the mick out of me and I take the mick out of him. It's a lovely show to do.'

For Daniel, *Midsomer Murders* has provided a passport to high-street recognition. Whereas John Nettles was a star returning to the limelight as Inspector Barnaby, the prime time exposure offered by Sgt Troy was a major career boost for Daniel.

Born in Stockton-on-Tees, Daniel began acting as a teenager, when two girls at school suggested he joined their youth theatre group because they needed more boys in the team. 'My friend, Damien, and I went along one week, but it wasn't really Damien's scene. I went back the following week and they were casting for *Bugsy Malone*.' For his audition Daniel recited Mark Antony's 'Friends, Romans, Countrymen' speech. 'I had no idea what you were supposed to do. My English teacher said, for an audition, I should probably do some Shakespeare. You can imagine how hilarious it must have been to see a 14-year-old standing there talking about the ills of the world, the ravages of time and all that.' It was clearly impressive all the same because he secured the lead role and from the first night he knew that acting was what he wanted to do. 'I said my first lines, walked on stage and immediately felt at home. It's a strange feeling to suddenly be in a place where everything feels comfortable and right.'

> 'I've had him fall in love with a couple of the murderers.'

Daniel then joined Stockton Youth Theatre, where he turned professional. After a few years performing and winning awards at the Edinburgh Fringe Festival, he was spotted by playwright John Godber, who was keen to take one of the plays on tour. That happened three weeks after Daniel graduated in English Literature from Durham University. He'd also secured an agent while still a student. 'I did a play called *I Hate Hamlet*, which was directed by Josh Andrews, son of Anthony Andrews, who came to see it and recommended me to his agents. They took me on and brought a few casting directors to see the play.' One of these was casting at the time for an ambitious Peter Flannery drama called *Our Friends in the North*. After half a dozen auditions, Daniel was offered the part of Anthony Cox, a headstrong young policeman from a broken family, a role that brought him alongside one of his heroes, Christopher Eccleston. 'Chris had just done that

Troy proves he's not always a bad driver in 'Dead Man's Eleven'.

death scene in *Cracker*, which I thought was amazing. I watched that with my dad and mentioned how much I'd love to work with him. Three months later I was – my first television job and it was absolutely incredible.' The rest of the cast was equally inspiring. 'Those four main characters: Chris, Gina McKee, Mark Strong and Daniel Craig are all lovely actors and they've all gone from strength to strength since. Peter Vaughan's study of Alzheimers was an incredible performance. At university, I was probably one of the most experienced theatrically, whereas now I felt like the young one, and it was a really nice feeling to be able to learn from other people again. It was exactly the way I had dreamt of the start of my career.'

Daniel then worked on episodes of *Peak Practice*, *The Bill* and *A Touch of Frost*, as well as playing Robbie Felton in *Catherine Cookson's The Wingless Bird*, before auditioning for a new one-off film called 'The Killings at Badger's Drift'. 'They didn't want to refer to it as a pilot,' he recalls. 'They thought it might go to a series but they said they were just thinking of it as a one-off film.' He met casting director Joyce Nettles, producer Betty Willingale and director Jeremy Silberston, read for the part of Sgt Troy and secured a second audition. 'That was lovely,' he remembers. 'I walked in and told the girl on reception I was there for the second audition but she couldn't find the list.' It turned out there wasn't one and he was the only actor being seen a second time. After the audition, he left the building, and immediately rang his agent to tell her it had gone well. She was already able to tell him he'd got the part. 'They'd rung up immediately I'd left the room.'

One of the first things Daniel did on accepting the role was to write himself a little history of Gavin Troy's life, so that he had something to refer to whenever Troy needed to act in a certain way. 'I like to do that when I build up a character,' he explains. 'So I know Troy plays five-a-side football with his friends on a Tuesday night. I know what GCSE results he got and I know he has three A-levels. They weren't brilliant grades but they were okay. He's quite a bright lad but didn't want to go to university. He wasn't into all that. I know his likes and dislikes, the kind of foods he eats, all that kind of stuff. It just allows you to get inside his shoes a bit.'

> *'He doesn't understand country folk and is often defensive because of that.'*

Some of this background comes from Caroline Graham's original novels, but a lot has been added, or altered, by Daniel. 'The characters are different,' he admits. 'When we started the series I was 24, so there's more of an age gap between him and Barnaby than in the books, which allows a tutor-pupil relationship to develop. Also, Troy's basically a Nazi in the books. As I play him, he does have lots of prejudices and also a naivety, a misunderstanding of people's situations. But he does learn and he is open to be proved wrong. In the books he is racist and sexist and homophobic, and every kind of 'ist' or 'ic' you can think of. That's easy to play but it's difficult to sustain. There need to be more human characteristics.'

Daniel sees Troy as an outsider who is unsure how to react in certain circumstances. 'He is a townie and proud of it. He doesn't understand country folk and is often defensive because of that and aggressive at times. It's a reaction to being looked at in a funny way. He moved down from the North when he was 11, that's why he's got a northern accent, which I soften a little.'

'I know that Troy watches *Hill Street Blues* on the re-run channels, and he watches *The Bill* and *The Vice*, because he thinks that's pretty cutting edge. He watches every police show and models his style on policemen he has seen on television. He absolutely loves being a policeman. He loves the glamour of it and the power he can sometimes have. The moment he has someone beneath him, he uses that power to the fullest extent and loves every single second of it. But I think he's a deeply moral person. He doesn't come across as it, but I think he is. That's why he's a policeman. He believes in right and wrong. Sometimes he lacks communicative skills. He tries to say something but it comes out all wrong. A lot of the time he's not far away from being right in the investigations and I think

Barnaby is unfair to him and patronizes him hugely. I also think he looks up to Barnaby, but he'd never in a million years admit it, and he finds him ridiculously politically correct at times.'

Troy is also a notoriously reckless driver. 'I love the driving scenes,' says Daniel, 'and I get to do some of the stunts. I don't think Troy is a particularly bad driver: he's just careless. He's had all the police training but his mind wanders. It's consistent with the rest of his character.' Daniel particularly enjoys working out the stunts. 'You're never in danger of hitting each other because you and the stunt man driving towards you both have a stop point. The camera will be behind either you or him so there's a foreshortening effect making it look much closer than it is. If the stunt isn't going to work for any reason you both stop at your stop point and start again. I'd like to do even more stunts but, obviously, for insurance purposes, I'm not allowed to.'

White-knuckle car rides have been carried over from the books but another obvious feature has been left out of the TV adaptation. On the written page Troy is a frustrated smoker, but Daniel doesn't smoke and never has done, so out went the cigarettes. 'I don't think the smoking particularly adds anything to the character. It's a vice but there are other ways of showing you're stressed or frustrated or bored and it would have been really hard for a non-smoker to sustain the smoking through the series. There would have been terrible litigation if I'd suddenly developed cancer at the age of 45 having consistently smoked whatever they'd given me!'

'He's in love with Cully. He always will be. The first time they met he fell for her.'

Another piece of Troy's baggage to be dumped for television was his fractious marriage, although he did wear a wedding ring in the earliest episodes. 'That was my fault for reading the books,' Daniel admits. 'It wasn't specified that they wanted him single, so I went with what I read in the book. It was a production decision to lose the ring. They said he was too young to be married. I could justify it by saying it was his grandmother's ring, but it disappeared very, very quietly. It was one of those early wrinkles that needed to be smoothed out.'

That doesn't mean that Troy has shied away from romance. He's a womanizer in the books and Troy still has an eye for the ladies. There were early signs that he had designs on Cully Barnaby, but Daniel denies that this was a conscious attempt to underline Troy's single status after the disappearance of the wedding band. 'I think they always intended him to be single but they never said anything. He's in love with Cully. He always will be. The first time they met he fell for her. He thought she was absolutely fantastic. He's impressed by the fact that she's an actress and she is clever. He finds strong women very attractive. That's probably because he was brought up by his mam and she's been a huge influence on his life. There's also the fact that Cully's unobtainable and she's the boss's daughter. There's something nice about getting one over on the boss. Troy can't very often get one over on him in policing terms but he certainly can as a young man. But I don't think Cully's ever given him a second thought, to be honest. The last thing she wants to do is go out with a policeman after seeing what her mam's been through.'

Daniel believes Troy and Cully could have a friendship but that Barnaby would not be happy with his bag carrier always coming to the house. 'I

The romantic side of Troy: infatuated with WPC Jay Nash (Gillian Kearney) in 'Dark Autumn'.

think he likes Troy and sees some potential in him but I don't think they ever would socialize. He's much younger and they don't have an enormous amount in common. With any relationship that's based on working closely together for that amount of time, you're not necessarily going to be friends but you'll get to know each other very well. The two come from entirely different philosophical standpoints. Troy has his ideas on policing and Barnaby has his own. It is a nice tension because you have two very different people working together towards the same goal.' Daniel considers that, although Troy is learning from him, he's never going to be the same kind of instinctive policeman as Barnaby. 'He's still going to have those prejudices. He's still going to think that these people who live in big houses have a chip on their shoulder. That's actually his chip. He goes in with a certain attitude that immediately causes people's hackles to rise.'

Daniel concedes that Troy has mellowed as the character has come into his own. 'The series began as a programme with John Nettles in the lead, then they saw how I play things and started to write for me. At the start, you follow the guidelines you've been given but, as you begin to understand the character, you tend to build it up yourself. You see certain directions you can go in and more interesting ways of playing it. It's easy to play an off-hand sidekick but it's more interesting to see someone who is developing, and more real to see a person develop as a result of working with someone who is better, or more experienced, than them.'

Because of this there were a few things in the scripts in series two and three to which Daniel objected. 'I said, hang on, we can't just keep Troy exactly the same as he's always been, because he has to develop. How did he ever get to detective sergeant if he's not going to develop further? And just from a natural process of growing up, you learn things. I didn't want to make Troy stupid. I wanted him to be green and inexperienced, as opposed to silly; young and immature, as opposed to deeply prejudiced and offensive.'

> 'I didn't want to make Troy stupid. I wanted him to be green and inexperienced, as opposed to silly.'

One of Troy's failings is that he can be deflected from the matter in hand. 'I've had him fall in love with a couple of the murderers, for instance,' says Daniel. 'He is blinded by beauty sometimes. We've also highlighted a lot of the comic aspects – how serious Troy can be in certain situations, or how he gets in a flap and doesn't know where the hell to put himself.'

Daniel does have a favourite episode. 'I enjoyed "Dark Autumn" because it gave me the chance to do something different from just asking questions or pontificating wrongly about aspects of an investigation,' he explains. 'It was nice to look at the personal aspect of Troy's character.' It was in 'Dark Autumn' that the first major romantic link was established for Troy, when he took a shine to WPC Jay Nash, and Daniel would like to see Jay return at some point. 'It's an interesting story line for Troy and Gillian Kearney is a fabulous actress. There was a genuine affection between the two characters so there is scope for her to come back and for them to have some kind of relationship, or at least a deeper friendship.' This episode illustrates how easily Troy can be distracted. 'When she's in danger, he's in danger of losing control. It's only a short moment but it makes him real and human, and you see beneath that cocky exterior.'

Daniel doesn't see much of Troy in himself. 'I do look very much like him,' he jokes, 'and I'm enthusiastic about life like he is but I hope I'm a lot brighter. I like football like him but I'm interested in all the arty-farty things in life and he isn't – at all. I think he's quite comfortable with his own life and I'm quite comfortable with mine.'

Daniel comes from a talented family. His father, Luke Casey, used to work on *Nationwide* and *The Money Programme* and now presents *North East Tonight* and *The Dales Diary* for Yorkshire-Tyne-Tees. 'My dad is one of my biggest heroes,' Daniel admits. 'That's where we get our interest in literature from.' By we, he refers to his four siblings. One of his sisters, Siobhan, is also a TV journalist, while another sister, Nula, writes music. He himself is musical. He sings and played violin for eight years. Now he's learning the guitar. Daniel is also quite sporty. 'I go to the gym three times a week and regularly run 5 or 6 miles. Running gives you a little bit of time inside your own head, especially if you've got something to think through, like a script.' Horse riding is another passion. 'I learned to ride when I was 18 months old on a little Shetland pony called Marcus', he mentions. 'That's one of the frustrations of *Midsomer Murders*. Troy's got to be frightened of horses but I love them. I'd love to do something where I could swash and buckle a bit on a horse.'

Since starting a new life as Gavin Troy, Daniel has also appeared in the drama series *The Grand*. 'I did two episodes with Jane Danson, who went on to *Coronation Street*', he recalls. 'I was playing a posh boy, who, again, was quite naive. I've got that sort of open face. I think it would be really interesting to cast me as a serial killer because you wouldn't suspect him at all.' But it is still as the sulky sergeant that he is recognized on the streets. 'I remember once being on the tube,' he says. 'There was a group of Arsenal fans, absolutely hammered. They were punching each other in the mouth and laughing about it. One of them

started to stare at me and I thought "Oh, here we go". He kept looking and looking, then he came over and said: "You're in that *Midsomer Murders*, ain't yeh? I love that programme, mate. You play a really good part. You're very funny." Then they all got off.'

As for *Midsomer Murders*, he appreciates the way the series has not been an overnight success. 'It's been a slow burner. It's taken a while to seep into the national consciousness but I think it is there now. Because of this, I'm sure it'll stay longer in people's minds than something that's been a flash in a pan. The series works

because it doesn't pretend to be anything it isn't. It doesn't try to be cutting edge when it isn't. We've never rested on our laurels and the characters are played in a truthful way. If everything is played straight then it works. It's like *The X-Files*. As long as you believe in that world that you're trying to create then people will believe in it when they're watching it. That's what television and drama are about: the suspension of disbelief.'

'There's also a little bit of magic sometimes. The relationship between me and John works very well: I think it's a good double act. I didn't meet John until the read-through. Which is really odd because, if you look at the series now, there's a real spark, a chemistry between us. It wasn't necessarily going to work, especially as I hadn't met him, but it did.'

Profile: DS Gavin Troy

Detective Sergeant Gavin Troy is DCI Barnaby's right-hand man. Some might prefer the terms sidekick, bag carrier or leg man, but perhaps the best description is pupil. Whereas Barnaby has years of experience and has seen it all before, Troy is decidedly wet behind the ears. There's no doubting his enthusiasm – except perhaps when fobbed off with disgusting jobs such as climbing down into a grave or collecting dog's vomit – but he has yet to acquire the skills of a mature detective and never fails to jump to simplistic conclusions. Frustratingly, on the rare occasion he does suggest a more fanciful solution to a case, his boss dismisses it in favour of the more down to earth. There's potential there, Barnaby can see that, but Troy needs to be knocked into shape and who better to do it than the fairest man in the Midsomer Constabulary? But even the fairest man finds Troy a touch irksome at times and can't resist a sarcastic dig at his partner's naivety or political incorrectness. For Troy does suffer from both these traits, although far better these than the bitterness and spite that define the Troy of the novels.

In Caroline Graham's writings, Troy is a man who thinks the world is against him. He deeply resents privilege, whether it is financial or educational, he can't resist a dig at the homosexual world or arty types, and he womanizes outrageously, even though he has a wife, Maureen, and a young daughter, Talisa-Leanne. If the TV Troy appears to have a chip on his shoulder, it is nothing compared to the plank carried around by his literary counterpart.

No, Troy as we see him is a different guy from the one we read about. For a start, he is not married. He also doesn't smoke, unlike the deeply addicted sergeant in the books. Physically his hair is floppy brown (shorter later), not bristly red. He is slim rather than thin, and he has an open face not a mean mouth. While always smartly presented at work, he is not as meticulous about his appearance as the book character. He also has a heart, an organ sadly missing from the Troy of the novels. If he is attracted to a girl – Cully, the 'guvnor's' daughter, perhaps, or WPC Jay Nash, or even an older woman – it is always with romance in mind, not just a crude one-night stand. One other key difference is that the Troy on television has mellowed. The odd sneer from the early days has been largely forgotten and he is more than ever keen to learn. While his sense of humour remains a little on the juvenile side, he appears to be maturing. The best he could offer in the early days, as he tried to exert some authority, was a feeble echo of his boss's own words, and, sometimes out of his depth, he was known to panic. Now, however, he's more confident and has begun to take the initiative. If this extracts the odd compliment from Barnaby, then all the more gratifying, but he holds his breath in case his boss is merely patronizing him – again. Should the opportunity arise to get one over on his boss, he does so with relish, but not triumphalism – an emotion more familiar to the Troy of the books. He is a reckless driver, but it is more a result of loss of attention than the boy racer mentality affecting the original Troy. Narrow escapes on the road certainly put grey hairs on the head of his superior, but Barnaby does appear to be warming to the lad. He will never embrace him with open arms, but he appears to enjoy his company more than in the first ever episode when he tells wife Joyce that Troy is not the sort of person she would want to meet!

Actor Daniel Casey has his own ideas of the character's upbringing, education and pastimes, some aspects of which are yet to manifest themselves televisually. But we do know that Troy was a pupil of Causton Comprehensive between 1983 and 1990 and, to supplement his education, later signed up for night classes in Spanish. He is sporty and a keen cricket fan. He takes a mountaineering holiday in Norway, but then strangely develops a fear of heights a few years later (perhaps the mountains were a bit too high). His mum is a big fan of the Edwardian Lady collection but he's not impressed when someone tries to sell him the *Country Diary* in the middle of October. Very little is seen of Troy's home life. In fact the only part of his house ever seen is his bedroom, where a large *X-Files* poster hangs above his bed.

Additional information from the pages of the novels fills in more of Troy's identity. We are told his contempt for privilege stems from the fact that his mother had to clean for a lady to make ends meet and that he was forced to wear posh hand-me-downs when he was a child. Of his father, little is revealed, except that he was a drunk. Troy lives with Maureen and Talisa-Leanne at 18 Russell Avenue, a small, terraced house they share with a former police German Shepherd dog (Troy loves dogs). He has been in the force for more than 10 years and worked with Barnaby for at least nine. On the case, he wears steel-rimmed glasses for driving. Despite all he has witnessed, he has no respect for the dead, yet remains a mass of insecurities and is prone to sulk when disciplined or proved wrong. A philistine by nature, he scoffs at the arts, but keeps a soft spot for TV costume dramas. Likewise, he eats like a glutton but knows no culinary refinement. By the time of Caroline Graham's latest novel, *A Place of Safety*, he is aged nearly 30.

Horse whispers: while Troy is nervous with horses, Daniel would love to ride again.

Jane Wymark is Joyce Barnaby

'There are very few similarities between myself and Joyce,' says Jane Wymark. 'I just wish I was as nice a person.' This is particularly hard on Jane because there can be very few people in real life as selfless and understanding as Joyce Barnaby. No wonder Tom adores her. But Jane does have someone in mind when playing the part. 'Ironically, I have an Auntie Joyce who is the most wonderful woman in the world – not in the "yucky" sense, but a very positive person. I found her terribly helpful as a role model for Joyce Barnaby, who is incredibly caring and kind. She's supportive and loving of both her husband and her daughter, although she is a bit long-suffering about his devotion to work. It's quite hard to play someone that decent sometimes, but I think I have become a nicer person as a result.'

Jane, whose father was the late Patrick Wymark, huge star of the series *The Power Game* in the 1960s, graduated in Drama and Theatre Arts from Birmingham University in 1973. Patrick died before she began her career but she does credit her father for introducing her to the acting world. 'It's likely I became an actor because of him,' she says. 'I grew up around the theatre and just loved the atmosphere, the magic.' Jane's television work in the run-up to *Midsomer Murders* was extensive and varied. Roles such as Diana in *Rob Roy* and Morwenna Chynoweth in *Poldark*, along with parts in *Rooms*, *Beasts* and *The Bass Player and the Blonde*, brought her to viewers' attention in the 1970s. More recent credits have included parts in *Seconds Out*, *Lovejoy*, *Drop the Dead Donkey*, *Maigret*, *A Fatal Inversion*, *Between the Lines*, *The Peter Principle*, *Pie in the Sky*, *A Touch of Frost*, *Dangerfield*, *No Bananas*, *Giving Tongue* and *Underworld*.

'It's quite hard to play someone that decent sometimes, but I think I have become a nicer person as a result.'

Jane remembers being interviewed by producer Betty Willingale, director Jeremy Silberston and casting director Joyce Nettles just after she'd been shopping for dressing gowns for her sons – a very Joyce-like activity. 'I turned up with these huge carrier bags, so there were plenty of jokes about that. It was a very friendly interview.' The next step towards making the role her own was a meeting with John Nettles. 'I had worked with John on a terrible film a little while before, so it wasn't that we were strangers. However, they needed to see how well we got on together, so we went to see him in his dressing room at the Barbican where he was appearing in a play. We had a good laugh.'

As Joyce only features in a limited number of scenes in each episode of *Midsomer Murders*, Jane does admit to finding the role a little frustrating at times. 'But they do occasionally let me out of my hutch so I can have some fun,'

she laughs. 'It's a shame the domestic scenes are often cut, but gauging the length of a two-hour film is very difficult and you can't let the plot go. I think the best episodes are the ones where the family is strongly involved, and especially if they're involved in the plot – that way they can't cut us out!' For this reason, and also because of its wonderful story line, she cites 'Judgement Day' as her favourite episode.

'Death's Shadow' is another of Jane's favourites, thanks to the presence of Richard Briers. 'The guest stars are amazing,' she says. 'When I go to the read-through and see the faces…'. Possibly her greatest thrill came in the pilot episode when she was cast opposite the late Rosalie Crutchley. 'I'd known her all my life,' Jane explains. 'I felt really honoured to be in a programme with her.'

About half of Jane's working year is now spent helping aspiring actors. 'I take workshops and I'm a tutor at the Guildhall School,' she reveals. 'I really enjoy it. I've even considered taking a PGCE so I could teach drama in secondary schools. Not long ago I also did an Arthur Miller play with inmates of HMP Latchmere in Richmond, which was a thrilling, wonderful experience.'

Jane sings in choirs, too – another link to Joyce Barnaby, who, in Caroline Graham's original novels, was once a professional singer. But she's always looking for opportunities. 'Offer me a playground and I take it,' she says.

In the meantime, she's happy to return to *Midsomer* and re-join the happy team. Not being in every scene, Jane only works for about a week on each episode, but doesn't feel like an outsider. 'It's strange in that I'm "family" so to speak, having been there from the start, but I'm also not around that much. It means I can stand aside a little and get a clear view of how things are going. If I go back and see people looking tired, I start feeling "mumsy" and feel I ought to run around looking after them.'

Jane also confesses to taking a little maternal pride in her on-screen daughter, Laura Howard. 'I went with Daniel to see Laura in *The Taming of the Shrew* in Richmond and I did feel very proud of her.' You could almost hear Joyce saying the same thing about Cully.

> *'the best episodes are the ones where the family is strongly involved, and especially if they're involved in the plot.'*

Profile: Joyce Barnaby

Behind every successful man…. The old adage could well have been coined in celebration of Joyce Barnaby, the ultimate supportive wife. It really cannot be much fun not knowing whether your husband is going to show up for an important social event, or to see him leave the dinner table early, but Joyce bears it all so gracefully. Not that Tom needs much of an excuse to put down his knife and fork and make for the door, because Joyce, for all her many positive attributes, is, frankly, a lousy cook. Her kitchen activities are not short of adventure, but the end result is invariably the same: disaster. She, herself, is strangely blind to her inadequacy in this department but Tom is not alone in fearing her output. Cully, too, quakes at the thought of her mother brandishing a saucepan, to the point where she sneaks chicken and ham pies into the house to supplement their diet.

Joyce may be to cookery what Troy is to driving proficiency, but otherwise she is a saint. She hardly ever quibbles when Tom is dragged away from home, or when he frets about his latest case; she is always there to keep the house together and accompany her husband when social occasion demands. This is her role in life, a role she has adopted since marriage and the birth of Cully – the devoted wife and mother (and indeed daughter, having once moved out for a couple of weeks to care for her own sick mother). Joyce and Tom were married in a

registry office, while Tom was investigating a case in London ('the Pimlico Poisoner'). To make amends for a disrupted honeymoon, he treated her to a romantic trip on the Orient Express for their silver wedding anniversary.

Though seldom grumbling about her lot, it does seem that Joyce has found her position a little frustrating at times. Perhaps that is why she attended an assertion training course at The Lodge of the Golden Windhorse at one point. Now that Cully has flown the nest, Joyce does have more time to spend on herself. She still enjoys amateur dramatics, working as costume designer and bit-part actor for the Causton Players, and is always keen to pick up new hobbies, from jam making, pottery and brass rubbing to running the croquet stall at a fête. Gardening is important in her life and she was thrilled to step out of Tom's shadow to judge the Perfect Village competition for *Country Matters* magazine. Indeed, she has always had an affinity with the country, and at one time was keen to move out of Causton and into the surrounding villages, until Tom

The supportive wife.

reminded her of what that might entail! Possibly her greatest attribute, however, is her down-to-earth common sense. When Tom is completely baffled over his latest mystery, some simple logic or a chance remark from Joyce may well provide the key to unlock the case.

Kitchen calamities are a hang-over from Caroline Graham's novels and Joyce is remarkably like her literary namesake: a good listener and a self-sacrificer of the highest order. In the books, we are told that she is aged 46 at the outset and used to be a professional singer. She trained at the Guildhall School of Music and was once a member of the chorus at the Royal National Opera House before giving it all up to look after the family. Now she teaches singing. Well, with Tom's job crippling their domestic life, someone must maintain harmony in the marriage.

Laura Howard is Cully Barnaby

There's a subtle difference between Laura Howard and Cully Barnaby, her *Midsomer Murders* persona. They are both devoted to the theatre and are up and coming actresses, but, whereas Cully only manages to scratch a living from the odd play or a TV commercial, Laura is rarely out of work.

Laura made her debut in the BBC sitcom *So Haunt Me*, in which she played teenager Tammy Rokeby alongside Tessa Peake-Jones and Miriam Karlin. That was when she was just 13 and acted under her real name of Laura Simmons. Because there was already an actor with the same name in Equity, she later adopted an old family name as her new surname and became Laura Howard. She has since starred as Deborah Briggs in *Soldier, Soldier*, *Cold Enough for Snow* and *Eskimo Day*, fitting in guest appearances in programmes such as *The Bill* and *Casualty* along the way.

'Cully is not that removed from me,' Laura explains. 'She's a young jobbing actress and we're the same basic type of person.' Laura also appreciates how the role may be small but can be very important. 'What Cully does is show Barnaby's home life and what makes him human,' she says. 'It's a great job.'

Cully has not appeared in every *Midsomer Murders* episode. She was omitted completely from series four and five, owing to Laura's theatre commitments. But the good news is that she is on her way back to Causton, which means that Barnaby will have his family close around him and poor old Troy can once again gaze and hope.

Profile: Cully Barnaby

Cully Barnaby is the apple of her dad's eye. The only child of Tom and Joyce, she has grown up attractive, confident and kind. When we first meet her, she has abandoned her rebellious days of bizarre-coloured hair and off-beat fashions and is a student at Cambridge. She is studying art history but is thinking of changing course because of her fascination with drama. She has just landed a major role in the John Ford play, *'Tis a Pity She's a Whore*, and is clearly eyeing a career in the theatre. By the time of the next episode, she has graduated, turned professional and is heading off to Poland with a Shakespearean group, leaving her cat, Kilmowski, to be cared for by mum and dad. With work at a premium, she returns to Causton at the time of the Causton Players' version of *Amadeus* and takes a shine to Nicholas Bentley, an up and coming star of the troupe. He is still her boyfriend several episodes later, when Barnaby consents to his shadowing Troy as research for a role he has picked up in a TV police series, but that is the last we see of Nico. In his absence, Troy is more than pleased to enjoy her occasional friendship, but for Cully the relationship will never develop further.

Me and my girl: Barnaby puts his daughter on the stage.

As much as she adores her father, Cully is less resigned than her mum to the strains his job places on domestic life. When Joyce goes to care for her sick mum for two weeks, Cully offers to look after Tom, only to find that being a policeman's wife means nothing but disrupted mealtimes and broken appointments. But she cares deeply for her dad, to the point where, on another occasion, she insists he lose weight and shackles him to a cruelly meagre diet. To keep him on the straight and narrow, she has to lie about the TV commercial she has just made for a chocolate gateau. Her acting work is sporadic and still, occasionally, brings her back to Causton. She once appeared in a version of *The Importance of Being Earnest*, at the Corn Exchange, attended a drama workshop in the town and then decided to write a history of the Causton Playhouse. Her agent, we discover, is named Peter Jackson.

Helping mum and dad house hunt in 'Dead Man's Eleven'.

Cully has not been seen for several episodes but is due to return to Causton, although her theatrical days will appear to be behind her. While 'resting' she will take a job with the local library service, which may prove useful in supplying leads for her father's investigations. She won't live at home, but will have her own flat in Causton.

Caroline Graham's picture of Cully is subtly different to the TV adaptation. While her interest in drama remains paramount, and she is just as devoted a daughter, Caroline's Cully does have a few rougher edges. She is tall, slim, dark-featured and, in her wacky fashions and strident hair colours, strikingly beautiful. Although she is without doubt a generous person, her tongue is sometimes less charitable than it should be. Always headstrong, she was taking the pill when aged 16 and, her father regrets, soft drugs during her punk era. A former pupil of Causton Comprehensive, she studies at New Hall, Cambridge, and joins Footlights, until becoming a professional actress. She has been fascinated with the theatre since she attended her first pantomime, aged four. She marries Nico but Tom fears that the relationship cannot last – can there really be room for two such egos in a marriage?

Barry Jackson is Dr Bullard

Barry Jackson likens his involvement in *Midsomer Murders* to that of a genuine pathologist. 'I just turn up for the odd day here or there, to inspect a dead body,' he says. 'My role is very real in that sense.'

Barry has played forensic pathologist Dr George Bullard since the very first episode but has only been seen in a handful of scenes throughout the entire run of the series. It doesn't leave much room for strong characterization but Bullard nevertheless comes across as a likeable, mature fellow, who, like his good mate Barnaby, is never blasé about the horror of his work. A few things have changed since Bullard's first appearance, however, as the pathologist's role has been brought up to date. 'In the pilot, Bullard turned up with a Gladstone bag,' recalls Barry. 'Then we realized that pathologists don't operate like that anymore.' Hence the clinical white suits Jackson dons in more recent episodes. The location for the numerous autopsies has also changed. 'We used a real mortuary once,' says Barry, 'but the smell was absolutely disgusting. Now we use a set that is also used by other series, such as *Silent Witness*, but it is always very cold.'

> 'We used a real mortuary once ... but the smell was absolutely disgusting.'

The role of Bullard is just one of dozens that Barry has taken on board during a long career. In the 1960s he led a dual life: acting under his own name and also working as a fight arranger under the name of Jack Barry. However, planning scraps and duels for series such as *Adam Adamant Lives!* became more demanding and Barry had to choose which career path to follow. 'The fight arranging started to take off and I had to decide whether to be rich or carry on being an actor. The people who took over the fight business became very wealthy but I wouldn't like to be involved with it these days. They don't seem to have enough time. I always used to insist on rehearsals, but today they just have to get on with it.'

Not that focusing on the dramatic side has proved to be a mistake. Barry's portfolio lists some of the biggest programmes in the history of British television, including *Cathy Come Home*, *Z Cars*, *A Family at War*, *Softly, Softly*, *Blake's 7*, *Poldark*, *The Professionals*, *Heartbeat*, *Casualty*, *All Creatures Great and Small*, *Minder*, *A Touch of Frost* and three visits to *Doctor Who*. The list also features *Bergerac*. 'I played a swine of a copper who chucked Jim out of his office,' Barry laughs. He and John Nettles happily see more eye to eye this time around.

Profile: Dr George Bullard

The reliable Dr Bullard is one of Barnaby's closest allies. The two men are of similar age and Bullard and his GP wife, Catherine, are family friends of Tom and Joyce. As forensic pathologist – one of the very few members of Barnaby's police support unit – it is Bullard's job to inspect the body at the scene of crime, provide immediate thoughts as to the cause of death and then thoroughly investigate the case through a port mortem examination. Like Barnaby, Bullard doesn't take death lightly and, while seldom distressed at the horrific things he sees, is always saddened by the cruelty before him. His mature approach contrasts sharply with that of his locum, Dan Peterson. When Bullard heads for Corfu for a well-earned break (actor Barry Jackson was touring with a play), Peterson, his junior, steps into the breach. For Peterson, the best way to cope with the trauma of such gruesome events is through flippancy and black humour – an approach that immediately rankles with Barnaby.

The Bullards have also found themselves to be victims on one occasion. In 'Faithful Unto Death', they admit to Barnaby that they, too, have invested in the failed mill arts venture which lies at the heart of the trouble in the village of Morton Fendle where they live (and where George is part of the bell-ringing team). In Caroline Graham's novels, however, Bullard lives in a hamlet called Charlecotte Lucy, close to Midsomer Worthy. He also has a grandchild, provided by his daughter, Karen, who is slightly younger than Cully, but his wife is not named. He spent years as the police surgeon before moving into his current role. In a typographical slip, he is referred to as 'Jim' Bullard in the book *Death of a Hollow Man*.

Haven't We Seen You Before?

Nico (Ed Waters) gets close to Cully.

'I had an interesting idea for *Midsomer Murders* that had never been done on television before, to my knowledge,' reveals Anthony Horowitz. 'Because we were talking about this very small county with little villages, I felt that the people in these villages would know each other and would turn up in different stories.' Anthony therefore wrote in parts for a small core of recurring characters who joined a few other colleagues and professionals in supporting Barnaby and Troy. Anthony claims that nobody ever noticed their re-appearance, but fans beg to differ.

PC Kevin Angel (Neil Conrich)

'The Killings at Badger's Drift'; 'Written in Blood'; 'Death of a Hollow Man'; 'Death's Shadow'; 'Strangler's Wood'; 'Beyond The Grave'

PC Angel's finest hour came in 'Beyond The Grave'. By taking a Civil War tour of Aspern Tallow, he was present at the discovery of the slashing of the portrait of Jonathan Lowrie, and was able to appraise the museum's security system before Barnaby arrived on the scene. Billed only as 'Duty Police Officer' for 'The Killings at Badger's Drift', the dependable copper gained his identity in 'Written in Blood' and was a reliable gopher for Barnaby and Troy in other early episodes.

Olive Beauvoisin (Eileen Davies)

'Death's Shadow'; 'Dead Man's Eleven'
Miss Beauvoisin made her *Midsomer Murders* debut as assistant to estate agent Ian Eastman but re-surfaced with her own Beauvoisin Estates agency in 'Dead Man's Eleven'. She is seen showing Joyce and Tom Barnaby around a cottage they are considering for their move out of Causton.

Nicholas Bentley (Ed Waters)

'Death of a Hollow Man'; 'Beyond the Grave'
Aspiring actor Nicholas Bentley is a much more prominent figure in Caroline Graham's novels than he is on television. (Anthony Horowitz was not keen on the character and refused to include him in his scripts.) As an up and coming star of the Causton Players, he meets Cully Barnaby during 'Death of a Hollow Man', and resurfaces as her boyfriend in 'Beyond The Grave', in which, having landed a part in a police soap opera, he asks to shadow Troy for research. In the books, however, Nico and Cully become engaged and marry. He wins a place at the National Theatre and is never tired of discussing his work, as Barnaby is wearily aware.

A familiar face in Badger's Drift: Christopher Villiers plays David Whitely.

Dr Catherine Bullard (Alwyne Taylor)

'Faithful Unto Death'; 'Beyond The Grave'
Catherine Bullard is never mentioned in the original Barnaby novels, but appears twice in the TV version. On the first occasion, in 'Faithful Unto Death', she is seen alongside her husband, George (the police forensic pathologist) as an investor in the mill crafts project, when it is revealed that she is also a local councillor. She re-appears in 'Beyond The Grave' when Barnaby takes advantage of the fact that she is the doctor in the village of Aspern Tallow. He calls on her ostensibly to receive treatment for an injury but also to glean some inside information about one of her patients.

Mrs Bundy (Marlene Sidaway)

'Written in Blood'; 'Death's Shadow'
Surely it is time Mrs Bundy was struck off the domestics' register. Anyone wishing to employ a housekeeper should steer clear of Mrs B, as she has an unfortunate habit of discovering dead bodies. Actress Marlene Sidaway has also featured in two other *Midsomer Murders* episodes: she appeared as a helpline counsellor in 'The Killings at Badger's Drift' and then played 1950s nanny Mrs Foster in the opening flashback sequence in 'Judgement Day'.

Dave Hedges (Jonie Broom)

'Death of a Stranger'; 'The Electric Vendetta'
First seen as an untrustworthy-looking friend of the accused Billy Gurdie in 'Death of a Stranger', lusty Dave Hedges moved from Marshwood to briefly re-appear in Midsomer Parva, for the episode entitled 'The Electric Vendetta'.

Charles Jennings (Terence Corrigan)

'Death's Shadow'; 'Dead Man's Eleven'
There is more to devious Charles Jennings than meets the eye. In 'Death's Shadow', the dark-haired 19-year-old is just one of the Badger's Drift villagers with a secret to hide. He returns in 'Dead Man's Eleven' as an odd-job man, working as a gardener and part-time barman at The Queen's Arms. He falls foul of his employer, Robert Cavendish, when he runs him out at cricket. For his sin, he is dropped from the Fletcher's Cross team and relegated to scorer.

James Jocelyne (Timothy Bateson)

'Written in Blood'; 'Death's Shadow'
Punctilious solicitor James Jocelyne, of Jocelyne, Tibbles and Delaney, has twice been called upon to provide evidence about his clients' personal and business affairs for Causton CID (three times, if you include 'Beyond The Grave', in which he was mentioned but not seen). A short, stocky man in late middle-age, he is described in the original novels as having a young family, much to Troy's surprise (and no little admiration).

Dan Peterson (Toby Jones)

'Strangler's Wood'; 'Dead Man's Eleven'; 'Death of a Stranger'; 'Judgement Day'
Dan Peterson is introduced in 'Strangler's Wood' as a junior who is standing in for George Bullard, who is holidaying in Corfu. Immediately, Barnaby takes a dislike to the flippant pathologist, not questioning his authority but objecting to his black humour and disrespectful approach to the job. The relationship mellows a little in later episodes, but there's never the same level of mutual respect that Barnaby and Bullard share, being of a similar age and each having served many years in the force.

Sebastian Renwick (Cyril Shaps)

'Strangler's Wood'; 'Blue Herrings'
In 'Strangler's Wood', Barnaby and Troy call at Renwick's jeweller's shop in the hope of identifying the owner of a Rolex watch found at the scene of a murder. Proprietor Sebastian Renwick is most helpful and shows them a log book that lists purchasers of such valuable items. The same character is seen again in 'Blue Herrings', when he is asked to buy a stolen watch. However, although Cyril Shaps again takes the role, the character is not listed as Sebastian Renwick, only as 'Jeweller'.

David Whitely (Christopher Villiers)

'The Killings at Badger's Drift'; 'Death's Shadow'
Randy estate worker David Whitely (spelt 'Whiteley' in the novel) is a key character in Barnaby's investigations in 'The Killings at Badger's Drift'. He reappears when Barnaby returns to the troubled village to plan his silver wedding anniversary celebrations in 'Death's Shadow'. The Tye estate having been sold for property development, Whitely is out of work and living in a caravan while reconstructing a cottage he has bought.

Most Welcome Guests

Finding all the wonderful guest stars that have left their thumbprint on *Midsomer Murders* was the responsibility of casting director Joyce Nettles for the first five series. The former wife of star John Nettles has worked on such notable dramas as *Inspector Morse*, *Kavanagh QC*, *Anna Karenina*, *Eskimo Day*, *Van der Valk* and the award-winning *Goodnight Mister Tom*, as well as alongside Brian True-May and Betty Willingale on *Harnessing Peacocks* and *The Vacillations of Poppy Carew*. But it was 10 years as head of casting at the Royal Shakespeare Company that stood her in very good stead for *Midsomer Murders*. 'I was there at a golden time and most of the people I worked with are now over a certain age, which is very handy considering the parts we have in the series,' she laughs.

> *There is no call for auditions for the major guest stars: their records speak for themselves*

Working mainly with Betty Willingale, Joyce has been responsible for casting most of the parts, except for the lead. 'John was cast before I came on board. That's common, for the main star to be cast by the producers. But we probably saw about half a dozen actors for Troy. I suggested Daniel, because we needed a very good young actor with a sense of humour.'

When it comes to guest stars, most of the suggestions for actors to fill roles have come again from Joyce, who reads the script and compiles a list of possibles for each character.

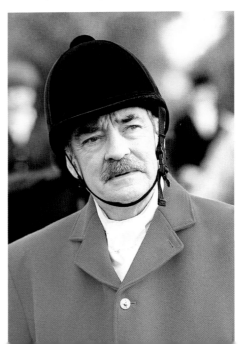

Larger than life: Richard Johnson as James Fitzroy in 'Death of a Stranger'.

'The list might have six names on it, or it might have 30,' she says. 'Then I go through the list with Betty and the director and decide to check the availability of three, or six, and we might make an offer at the same time.'

There is no call for auditions for the major guest stars: their records speak for themselves. Also, if the relationship between the casting director and producer is good, as between Joyce and Betty, trust develops and even some lesser-known performers are waved through on the recommendation of one or the other. Joyce tends to bring in the actors for the smallest parts and these sometimes have to read for the team, but it depends on how well she knows them. There are very few problems with actors failing to come up with the goods, as director Jeremy Silberston confirms. 'We set out to get actors of a high quality, and those people deliver,' he says. And the importance of good casting is not lost on any of the crew, as it affects the whole mood of the set. 'Casting have been very good about getting the right people for the job,' says stunt co-ordinator Colin Skeaping. 'So many times you go and work on something and you cannot believe the character because they've mis-cast the person.'

Angela Thorne and Anton Rodgers in 'Market for Murder'.

Actors are signed up about two months before production starts. 'They won't commit themselves any earlier,' Joyce explains. 'Scripts haven't been written and they don't want to be tied up in case another offer comes in.' Very few of the actors approached – perhaps half a dozen at most – have ever turned down a chance to appear in the series. That, according to Joyce, is largely down to John Nettles.

'John is a sympathetic lead. There are no "wobblies" or tantrums: he's easy to work with. Film sets can be grumpy or happy and that starts at the top. Also the guests are paid decent money, not vast amounts, but decent money. They are treated courteously, the food is good on set and the word gets out that *Midsomer Murders* is a nice programme to work on.' Producer Brian True-May agrees:

> '*I think people enjoy having something where you don't necessarily have to be hyper-real and you're not going for the* EastEnders *underplay. It gives actors the chance to explore and be large.*'

'Talented and well-known actors, classy actors like *Midsomer Murders* because they know they're going to get a big audience and have a bit of fun.' As Daniel Casey says: 'The series lends itself to British actors and all the characters, no matter how big or small, have their own little quirk or character point you can work on. I think people enjoy having something where you don't necessarily have to be hyper-real and you're not going for the *EastEnders* underplay. It gives actors the chance to explore and be large.' With each episode taking up to five weeks to film, Daniel feels there's enough time to give a good performance. 'You don't feel hurried. You have the chance to talk about the character and see how that character develops.'

He also gives great credit to Joyce Nettles. 'People trust her judgement. As an actor, when you go up for something and Joyce is casting it, you think, yeah, this is good.'

Having such big names as Richard Briers, Anna Massey and Robert Hardy on set certainly keeps the regular cast on their toes, but everyone is inspired by their presence, not intimidated. 'You can't be intimidated because this is what you've wanted to do since you were 14,' stresses Daniel Casey. 'You get the chance to act with people who are very, very good. I don't understand people who don't want to surround themselves with excellence because that can only make you better. It makes you concentrate harder, work harder and can only improve your performance.'

Phyllida Law as Felicity Dinsdale in 'Blood Will Out'.

'In the first episode of the series proper we had Anna Massey, Joanna David and David Troughton, just fantastic actors. I've got a huge amount of stuff in my armoury now that I'm going to use – just stolen from everyone I've worked with. I spent a lovely evening with Bernard Hepton telling me lots of stories about his time directing at the National, about *Tinker, Tailor, Soldier, Spy* and all his time in rep. What an amazing man: talented, very, very bright, and also unassuming. Some of those days and evenings are just priceless. The storytelling tradition is a vital part of your heritage as an actor. Some stories have been passed along and along, from Olivier and Gielgud and way before them, and the experience people like Bernard have gained as young actors from some of the greats, I'm now gaining from them. It's a lovely thought. Sometimes it's like being in a masterclass.'

Midsomer worthies (left to right from top): Larry Lamb, Imelda Staunton, Rosalie Crutchley, Kevin McNally, Nickolas Grace,

Josephine Tewson, Duncan Preston.

Daniel singles out Alan Howard for particular mention for his use of language and the way he successfully emphasizes parts of a word that other actors would never think of stressing. 'He is such a powerful character and a powerful talent. It's just wonderful being in the company of people who are at the top of their game and know what they're talking about. John [Nettles] was delighted that Alan did one episode and it was nice to see him looking at someone and thinking "Maybe I'll try that" – to see him learning as well.'

Richard Johnson was another larger than life guest. 'He treated John the way John treats me,' laughs Daniel. 'He called him "Johnny", treated him like the juvenile, which was hilarious.' And then there's Richard Briers, who insisted on doing his own stunts, including a leap from a church tower. 'He jumped off the roof on to scaffolding. The stunt man was there to catch him, but he still did it. He was fantastically game', Daniel recalls. 'He was determined to do it and nothing was going to stop him. It looks fantastic on film, to see him disappear off the edge.' Jane Wymark was another star who was impressed by Richard Briers's appearance. 'Richard told me he'd worked out "a bit of acting" for his big speech in "Death's Shadow". "When I do it," he said, "I'm not going to blink." And he never did. I watched him closely and he never blinked. Viewers probably didn't realize this but it subtly conveyed the idea that he had suddenly become a maniac.'

Above: Prunella Scales as Eleanor Bunsall in 'Beyond the Grave'.

Right: Wendy Craig as Victoria Bartlett in 'A Worm in the Bud'.

But the last words on the welcome guests has to go to lead man John Nettles, whose own character is so laid back that it makes all the visitors shine. 'Barnaby's the only normal person there, which gives a lot of scope for that host of English actors who are so wonderful at playing eccentricity. A lot of them turn out to be my chums so it's a bit like an old pals' club for me.'

A New Year in Midsomer: A Day on the Set

A wet morning in mid-May. Fifty people splash through the puddles and into The Green Room at Pinewood Studios. They've been called up for the read-through of the script for 'A Talent for Life' – the first episode in a new series of *Midsomer Murders*.

It's been six months since filming was last wrapped up and this is an opportunity for the crew to discover what everyone's been doing over the winter. Of the 'regular' actors, Jane Wymark is the first to arrive and does an excellent impression of Joyce Barnaby, playing the perfect host. Daniel Casey has commuted from Scarborough, where he has been starring in a play, and John Nettles is almost the last to show his face, looking anything but like the urbane Inspector Barnaby. He's grown a beard and sports denim shirt and jeans.

Meanwhile, the guest stars have also stepped out of the rain. Honor Blackman, Philip Franks, Amanda Root, Jeff Rawle, Susan Wooldridge and other familiar faces take their places around a long conference table. In the centre sit director Sarah Hellings, script editor Christopher Penfold and writer David Hoskins. Alongside them producer Brian True-May starts proceedings by welcoming back Laura Howard, whose character, Cully Barnaby, has not been seen for two series. Then it's into the script. The actors work their way through each scene, reading aloud their lines. It all goes remarkably smoothly, considering there have been no rehearsals. There are giggles when Daniel stumbles over a line and then starts reading John's part but, within an hour, it's all done and dusted. While most people wander off for a sandwich and coffee, the script team pore over the morning's work, re-working lines that sounded clumsy and shortening the odd speech. Now the make-up and costume departments spring into action, eyeing up their guests for future cosmetic treatment and whisking them away to the wardrobe wagon to try on outfits so-far prepared. Gradually, however, the crowd disperses, rehearsal schedules clutched in hand.

Two weeks later, the rain continues to fall, this time on the lawns of a country house in deepest Oxfordshire. The team has already been filming for a week and now they're staging a funeral. One of the principals has met a grisly end and is about to be given a rousing sendoff. At 8 am, Champagne (specially packaged ginger ale) is being lifted from the boot of a magnificent peacock blue Bentley and taken into the house as a group of sober-clad extras step nervously down the gravel drive, Barnaby and Troy bringing up the rear. The scene is filmed from countless angles. Lights are carefully positioned, then re-positioned, and track is laid for the camera to move around the action. There are hoots of laughter as the camera is suddenly derailed and director of photography Doug Hallows leaps clear. All the while the weather does its best to prolong the day. The crew battle through, make-up ladies Penny and Jeanette frantically spraying down wayward wisps of hair, John from wardrobe whipping away protective coats and umbrellas only seconds before 'action' is called. Sound recordist Richard Reynolds is wary of rain on the microphone and the proximity of the M40 motorway. Even though the house is idyllically situated amid timeless 'Midsomer' countryside, the rumble of the 21st century can still be heard. By keeping the microphone close to the performers, and aiming it in the right direction, however, tranquillity can be restored.

The rain falls harder over lunch. The extras huddle in the dining bus, balancing plates loaded up at the catering truck. Guest stars retire to cosy caravans that are divided into 'suites'. After lunch, the actors are ferried by car back to the house from the muddy farm field that acts as a base. Guest performer Peter Cellier stands on a balcony high above a sea of mourners that fill the entrance hall. His tribute speech to the dead party is filmed from above, below and through the crowd, which has been carefully choreographed to allow the camera easy access to Barnaby, Troy and the other stars. Actor Robert Putt carries a tray of oysters down a curved staircase, and offers Barnaby a taste. Their conversation is later filmed again separately, and from every possible direction. Intriguing snippets of chit-chat among other guests get similar treatment.

The real owner of the house pops by and reveals that the art department has brought in artefacts and old pictures that add depth to the character that 'lives' there. Her dogs have been running around all day, playfully sniffing at all the equipment and occasionally threatening to trot into the background of a shot. But it's not been a problem: it's a good-natured set.

By the end of the day only about two minutes of the episode is in the can. With better weather – and scenes with fewer actors and extras – other days will be more productive. Just as well: there are five, long months ahead for the team. It's still only May, but they're already deep into Midsomer.

Episode Guide

The following pages celebrate the 23 *Midsomer Murders* episodes so far recorded, in the order in which they first appeared on British television. They include synopses of the main story lines (without giving too much away!), full cast lists and major credits, plus bits of trivia and features on the leading guest stars in each episode. The transmission dates are for the first showings. At the time of going to press, the last four episodes had not been broadcast in the UK.

Regular Cast

DCI Tom Barnaby . . . . .John Nettles
DS Gavin Troy . . . . .Daniel Casey
Joyce Barnaby . . . . .Jane Wymark
Cully Barnaby . . . . .Laura Howard *
Dr George Bullard . . . . .Barry Jackson **

* all episodes except 'Garden of Death'; 'Destroying Angel'; 'The Electric Vendetta'; 'Who Killed Cock Robin?'; 'Dark Autumn'; 'Tainted Fruit'; 'Ring Out Your Dead'; 'Murder on St Malley's Day'; 'Market for Murder'; 'Worm in the Bud'

** all episodes except 'Strangler's Wood'; 'Dead Man's Eleven'; 'Death of a Stranger'; 'Blue Herrings'; 'Judgement Day'; 'The Electric Vendetta'; 'Ring Out Your Dead'; 'Murder on St Malley's Day'

Major Production Credits

Associate Producer . . . . .Patricia Greenland, Veronica Castillo,
Ian Strachan

Director of Photography . . . . .Nigel Walters, Chris O'Dell,
Graham Frake, Steve Saunderson

Production Designer . . . . .Don Giles, Jan Spoczynski,
Robert Foster

Art Director . . . . .Rachel Heady, Sandy Garfield,
Gina Stewart, Matthew Davies,
Andrijana Tovarloza, Bill Brown,
Deborah Morley

Editor . . . . Derek Bain

Composer . . . . Jim Parker

Costume Designer . . . . Reg Samuel

Make-Up Designer . . . . .Marilyn MacDonald, Caroline Noble,
Maggie Palphramand, Sally Harrison

Make-Up Artist . . . . Wendy Spriggs, Penny Bell

Location Manager . . . . Georgina True-May, Susie Booker,
Denis Firminger

Production Co-ordinator . . . . Julianne Long, Joanna Timms,
Pat Bryan, Sam Mill

Production Accountant . . . . .Vincent O'Toole, John Groves,
Steve Cronick

Casting Director . . . . .Joyce Nettles

Script Supervisor . . . . Ann Gallivan, Carol Gardner,
Anwen Bull

Visual Effects . . . . .Neal Champion, Stuart Brisdon,
Steve Lucas, Tony Harding

Stunt Co-ordinator . . . . .Dave Holland, Stuart St Paul,
Colin Skeaping

Sound Recordist . . . . .Les Honess, Ronald Bailey,
Maurice Hillier, Richard Reynolds

Costume Supervisor . . . . .Mary Judge, Abigail Hicks

Script Editor . . . . Mariana Mejia,
Christopher Penfold (ScriptWorks)

Executive Producer for A&E . . . . Delia Fine

Supervising Producer for A&E . . . . . . Kris Slava

The Killings at
Badger's Drift

Cast

Emily Simpson	Renée Asherson
Phyllis Cadell	Selina Cadell
Dennis Rainbird	Richard Cant
Lucy Bellringer	Rosalie Crutchley
Mary Sharp	Avril Elgar
Michael Lacey	Jonathan Firth
Henry Trace	Julian Glover
Barbara Lessiter	Diana Hardcastle
Katherine Lacey	Emily Mortimer
Terry Bazely	Cory Pulman
Iris Rainbird	Elizabeth Spriggs
Judith Lessiter	Jessica Stevenson
David Whitely	Christopher Villiers
Dr Trevor Lessiter	Bill Wallis
Anna Quine	Barbara Young
Vicar	Nigel Asbridge
Policeman	Paul Putner
Duty Police Officer	Neil Conrich
Counsellor 1	Peter Jordan
Counsellor 2	Marlene Sidaway
Counsellor 3	Jonathan Oliver
Giovanni	Simon Godwin

Credits

Writer	Anthony Horowitz
Novel	Caroline Graham
Producers	Betty Willingale, Brian True-May
Director	Jeremy Silberston
Transmitted	Sunday, 23 March 1997, 8–10pm ITV

Story line

Previous page: There's a shock in store for Emily Simpson (Renée Asherson) when she cycles to the woods in search of a rare orchid.

Elderly spinster Emily Simpson's venture into the woods around the village of Badger's Drift ('Midsomer's Best-Kept Village' on numerous occasions) proves to be a grave mistake. Searching for a rare orchid to upstage her life-long friend, Lucy Bellringer, Emily stumbles upon a terrible secret – an illicit love affair that would rebound shockingly should the truth ever be revealed. Terrified by the burden of her discovery, the retired teacher hurries away from the scene, only to die in suspicious circumstances at her Beehive Cottage later that evening. Enter Inspector Tom Barnaby and his sneering junior, Sgt Gavin Troy, of the Causton CID, charged with discovering the murderer. Their attention falls on a mixed bunch of villagers who appear to have something to hide. They include wheelchair-bound local squire Henry Trace, whose own wife died in suspicious circumstances only two years before; his frustrated sister-in-law Phyllis Cadell; Henry's youthful bride-to-be Katherine Lacey, and her artist brother Michael. Also in the frame are lusty estate manager David Whitely, nauseating Iris Rainbird and her creepy undertaker son, Dennis, who appear to live beyond their means, and the dysfunctional Lessiter family – dubious doctor Trevor, flighty wife Barbara and frumpy daughter Judith. Eventually, with more than one death to tax his brain, Barnaby's detection skills need to be sharply honed to penetrate the web of blatant deceit, closet skeletons and cold blackmail that wraps itself around the inhabitants of an apparently tranquil English village.

Rosalie Crutchley (Lucy Bellringer)

After a stage, film and small screen career which spanned some 60 years, the part of determined spinster Lucy Bellringer in 'The Killings at Badger's Drift' proved to be one of Rosalie Crutchley's last TV roles. She died in July 1997, four months after the film was transmitted. On television, Rosalie appeared in the BBC's 1970 adaptation of *Jane Eyre* and Granada's 1977 version of *Hard Times*, as well as alongside Patrick McGoohan in *The Prisoner* and Alec Guinness in *Smiley's People*. In 1971, she starred as Catherine Parr in the award-winning *Six Wives of Henry VIII*. By the time Barnaby beckoned, Rosalie had enjoyed plenty of experience alongside TV detectives, having featured in series such as *Cribb, Miss Marple, Agatha Christie's Poirot, Sherlock Holmes* and *Cadfael*.

Tea with the grotesque Iris Rainbird (Elizabeth Spriggs) holds little appeal for Barnaby and Troy.

Elizabeth Spriggs (Iris Rainbird)

Elizabeth Spriggs – regularly seen as a bold mother figure on television – has featured in numerous TV series over the years, including *The Glittering Prizes, Frost in May, Fox, Oranges Are Not The Only Fruit, Jeeves and Wooster, Martin Chuzzlewit, Middlemarch, Taking Over the Asylum* and *Simon and the Witch*. She is probably best known as Nan in *Shine On Harvey Moon* or Mrs Mullen in *Playing the Field*. However, her role in 'The Killings at Badger's Drift' was one of the most bizarre in her long TV career. The character of Iris Rainbird was a particularly grotesque creation – sickeningly gushing, unctuous, and

There appears to be a rare mistake in 'The Killings at Badger's Drift', when it is claimed that Wednesday's test match was rained off. In reality, test cricket is never played on Wednesdays in England. But who ever said Midsomer Murders was part of the real world?

poisonously nosy – wallowing in an extremely unhealthy relationship with her equally vile undertaker son.

Jessica Stevenson (Judith Lessiter)

Midsomer Murders provided an early insight into Jessica Stevenson's star potential. Her role as the plain, neglected daughter of Dr Trevor Lessiter, was recorded before she began work on the comedies *The Royle Family*, in which she played diet-dodging next-door neighbour Cheryl, and *Spaced*, in which she starred alongside Simon Pegg. Keen-eyed viewers may have also spotted Jessica in *The House of Eliott*, *Crown Prosecutor* and alongside comedians Harry Enfield and Armstrong and Miller.

Will Michael Lacey (Jonathan Firth) attend the wedding of his sister Katherine (Emily Mortimer) to Henry Trace?

Written in Blood

Story line

*Previous page:
Is Honoria
Lyddiard (Anna
Massey) about to
carve the Sunday
roast?*

There is a dilemma facing the members of the Midsomer Worthy Writers' Circle.
They plan to invite a celebrity author to address one of their meetings but cannot
decide on a suitable guest. Eventually it is agreed to ask Max Jennings,
blockbuster novelist, much to the obvious concern of the group's chairman,
reclusive widower Gerald Hadleigh. He refuses to send the invitation personally
and so it is left to the group's secretary, Causton Comprehensive's smug drama
teacher, Brian Clapper, to do the honours. On the day of the arranged meeting
Gerald confides in kind neighbour Amy Lyddiard that he and Max Jennings have
met before and that he doesn't want to be left alone with him. Amy agrees to act

as chaperon. A turbulent meeting takes place but, when the assembled party takes its leave, Max manages to slip back indoors, leaving Amy outside with her bullying sister-in-law, Honoria. The next day Gerald is found battered to death with a candlestick and Max Jennings, as Barnaby soon discovers, is nowhere to be found. Obvious suspects are the lecherous Brian, who has lied about his whereabouts after the meeting; his wife, Sue, who has been covering up for him, and local antiques dealer Laura Hutton, who had a crush on Gerald and has admitted wandering back to his house later that night. Amy and Honoria seem to be in the clear as they retired on returning home. However, there is something suspicious about the woman seen entering Gerald's home the night before the murder, as well as Max's drunken wife, Selina, and evasive secretary, Barbara Neale, who both appear to know more than they are letting on. Barnaby and Troy have a lot of digging to do and, when Max is found poisoned at a seaside holiday home, the pieces of the jigsaw seem further apart than ever.

Left: Brian Clapper (David Troughton) receives his comeuppance from Edie Carter (Nancy Lodder).

Opposite: Death in a writers' circle leaves our heroes wondering if the pen really is mightier than the sword.

Anna Massey (Honoria Lyddiard)

The character of Honoria Lyddiard, as described in the original novel by Caroline Graham, is a stout, powerful, muscular woman, not adjectives that immediately come to mind when considering Anna Massey. So it is all the more remarkable that the arrogance, malice and domineering nature of Honoria shine through her performance. This is, of course, the result of 40 years' experience in the theatre, in film and on television, which has taken in such series as *Rebecca*, *The Mayor of Casterbridge*, *Mansfield Park*, *Hôtel du Lac* (for which she claimed a BAFTA award), *Inspector Morse*, *A Respectable Trade* and *A Nice Day at the Office*. Anna's father was *Dr Kildare* star Raymond Massey, and her brother was the late Daniel Massey.

'Written in Blood' contains one of Midsomer Murders' *two pieces of overseas action: the opening flashback sequence is set in Durrow, Ireland, in 1955. It also includes the series' only visit to London.*

Una Stubbs (Selina Jennings)

Dancing with Cliff Richard in *Summer Holiday* is a long way from playing disillusioned, drunken wife Selina Jennings (who swims in her jewels, much to Troy's astonishment), but this *Midsomer Murders* role gave TV viewers a rare opportunity to see Una Stubbs in straight drama. Apart from dancing, most of her TV experience has been in comedy, particularly, of course, as Rita, the giggling daughter of Alf Garnett in *Till Death Us Do Part*, as Aunt Sally, the skittle doll, in *Worzel Gummidge*, and as a team captain in *Give Us a Clue*. Other parts have come in series such as *Fawlty Towers*, *Educating Marmalade*, *Keeping Up Appearances*, *Heartbeat*, *Morris Minor's Marvellous Motor* and *The Worst Witch*.

> '"When Written in Blood" came out, some critics didn't understand what we were trying to do,' reveals writer Anthony Horowitz, referring to comments made about the horror movie clichés he and Jeremy Silberston had built into the film. 'Of course it's *Psycho* and pure hokum – lighting flashing as the murderer comes up with a knife, that sort of thing. But we were revelling in the cliché. We were enjoying the fact that it was deadly daft.'

David Troughton (Brian Clapper)

Son of Patrick and elder brother of Michael, David Troughton is one of Britain's most popular character actors, excelling in loud but comically shallow creations such as Dr Bob Buzzard in *A Very Peculiar Practice* and drama teacher Brian Clapper here in 'Written in Blood'. His many other television appearances have come in programmes as varied as *Doctor Who*, *Our Mutual Friend*, *Wings*, *Backs to the Land*, *The Winslow Boy*, *David Copperfield*, *Wessex Tales*, *Cider with Rosie*, *Drop the Dead Donkey*, *Lloyd George Knew My Father*, *Madame Bovary*, *Undercover Heart*, *Underworld*, *Heartbeat* and *Kavanagh QC*.

> *Early* Midsomer Murders *episodes featured a special titles sequence, listing major credits alongside a series of vignettes of English village life. These have now been replaced by text overlays as the action unfolds.*

Cast

Laura Hutton	Jane Booker
Amy Lyddiard	Joanna David
Honoria Lyddiard	Anna Massey
Sue Clapper	Judith Scott
Max Jennings	John Shrapnel
Selina Jennings	Una Stubbs
Gerald Hadleigh	Robert Swann
Brian Clapper	David Troughton
Barbara Neale	Annoushka Le Gallois
Mrs Bundy	Marlene Sidaway
Mr Belgrove	John Bardon
James Jocelyne	Timothy Bateson
Miss Panter	Jacqueline Morgan
Boreham	Mark Bagnall
Edie Carter	Nancy Lodder
Tom Carter	Daniel Newman
Denzel	Marcus Rogers
Collar	Zoot Lynam
Liam Hanlon	Jay Barrymore
Liam's father	Murray Ewan
Mr Baker	Brian Parr
PC Angel	Neil Conrich
Policeman 2	Paul Putner
Policeman 3	David Maybrick
Barman	Bryan Burdon

Credits

Writer	Anthony Horowitz
Novel	Caroline Graham
Producers	Betty Willingale, Brian True-May
Director	Jeremy Silberston
Transmitted	Sunday, 22 March 1998, 8–10pm ITV

Death of a Hollow Man

Story line

Although 'Death of a Hollow Man' is the only Midsomer Murders screenplay written by Barnaby's creator Caroline Graham, some major changes to her own novel were made when it was brought to television, emphasizing the different demands of the medium. The character of Agnes Gray, for instance, does not appear in the book.

Preparations are well under way for the Causton Players' presentation of Amadeus at the town's Corn Exchange. Costumes are being prepared, sets finished, lines committed to shaky memory. But the performers and stagehands are not a congruous bunch. Arrogant lead man Esslyn Carmichael is having problems with his promiscuous young wife, Kitty, while his former wife, Rosa, is shredded by jealousy. When the curtain goes up on the first night, rivalries invade the plot, culminating in a gory climax involving a switch blade razor. As Esslyn takes his final bow a question is revealed: Who sabotaged the props? Could it have been pompous director Harold Winstanley, a man whose theatrical talents were surely wasted on this shambolic troupe? Or perhaps gay bookshop owner Avery Phillips or his partner, Tim Young, who has been behaving rather oddly of late? What about ambitious young actor Nicholas Bentley, or the close father and son pairing of Colin and David Smy who were, after all, well-placed behind the scenes? Surely dowdy stage manager Deirdre Tibbs could not be involved: her mind would have been too preoccupied with worries about her senile father. And what did the recent murder of Esslyn's cousin, Agnes Gray, have to do with proceedings? Lucky then that Chief Inspector Tom Barnaby is in the audience, to cheer along wife Joyce who has a small part in the production. The investigation into a particularly grisly murder can begin before the blood stops flowing.

Opposite: A 'hollow man' (Nicholas Le Prevost) has plenty to think about.

Left: Hell hath no fury ... scorned wife Rosa Carmichael (Sarah Badel) takes revenge on Kitty's car.

Cast

Rosa Carmichael . . . . . .Sarah Badel
Deirdre Tibbs . . . . . Janine Duvitski
David Smy . . . . Ian Fitzgibbon
Harold Winstanley .Bernard Hepton
Colin Smy . . . . .Geoffrey Hutchings
Tim Young . . . . .Richard Huw
Esslyn Carmichael . . . . Nicholas Le
Prevost
Doris Winstanley . .Angela Pleasence
Kitty Carmichael .Debra Stephenson
Nicholas Bentley . . . . . . .Ed Waters
Avery Phillips . . . . .Nick Woodeson
Agnes Gray . . . . .Denyse Alexander
Jenny Evers . . . . . . .Vivienne Moore
Mr Tibbs . . . . .John Cater
Mrs Maddox . . . . Hilary Crane
Charles Makepeace . Robert McIntosh
Peggy Marshall . .Patricia Heneghan

Emperor Joseph . . . Michael Cronin
PC Kevin Angel . . . . . .Neil Conrich
WPC Hitchens . . . . . .Megan Fisher
Becky Smith . . . . .Sonya Walger
Mr Green . . . . .Alan Leith
Elderly lady . . . . . .Elizabeth Tyrrell
TV announcer . . . . . Eunice Roberts
Constable . . . . .Iain Fraser
Solo voice . . . . .Catherine Bott

Credits

Writer . . . . Caroline Graham
Novel . . . . .Caroline Graham
Producers . . . . Betty Willingale,
Brian True-May
Director . . . . .Jeremy Silberston
Transmitted . . . . Sunday, 29 March
1998, 8–10pm ITV

Bernard Hepton (Harold Winstanley)

What has Tim (Richard Huw) been up to – and with whom?

The great Bernard Hepton puffed himself up wonderfully to fill the clothes of pompous theatre director Harold Winstanley in 'Death of a Hollow Man'. It was a role that contrasted notably with Bernard's earlier star performances, which had often been in dour and serious parts. They include the roles of Thomas Cranmer in *The Six Wives of Henry VIII*, the Kommandant in *Colditz*, Resistance operative Albert Foiret in *Secret Army*, secret agent Toby Esterhase in *Tinker, Tailor, Soldier, Spy* and vengeful Donald Stimpson in *The Charmer*. But the more comical aspects of Harold's character did have a precedent: Bernard also starred in the sitcom *The Squirrels* in the 1970s. Other credits have included *I, Claudius*, *Jane Austen's Emma*, *Sadie It's Cold Outside*, *Bleak House*, *The Troubleshooters*, *Blood Money* and *Bergerac*.

Faithful Unto Death

Cast

Alan Hollingsworth . . .Roger Allam
Doreen Anderson . . .Rosalind Ayres
Gray Patterson . . . . . .Mark Bazeley
Nigel Anderson . . . . . .Paul Brooke
Reg Buckley . . . . . . .Paul Chapman
Harry Vellacott . . . . . .David Daker
Felicity Buckley . . . .Michele Dotrice
Bunny Dawlish . . . . . . .Peter Jones
Sarah Lawton . . . .Tessa Peake-Jones
Vince Perry . . . . Andrew Powell
Brenda Buckley . . . . Sophie Stanton
Elfrida Molfrey .Eleanor Summerfield
Simone Hollingsworth . . . . . .Lesley
Vickerage

Catherine Bullard . . .Alwyne Taylor
Richard . . . . .Neville Phillips
Hermione . . . . Ann Queensberry
Freddy . . . . Tom Mullion

Credits

Writer . . . . .Douglas Watkinson
Novel . . . . .Caroline Graham
Producers . . . . . . .Betty Willingale,
Brian True-May
Director . . . . .Baz Taylor
Transmitted . . . . .Wednesday,
22 April 1998, 8–10pm ITV

Story Line

Previous page: The church at Little Marlow as used in 'Faithful Unto Death'.

In Caroline Graham's novel, the setting for 'Faithful Unto Death' is a village called Fawcett Green, not Morton Fendle.

Morton Fendle is not the happy community it appears to be. The village fête seems jolly enough but is soon marred by an ugly brawl. Tom Barnaby, taking tea with his family, is fortunately well placed to restrain the instigator, a serial womanizer by the name of Gray Patterson, as he attacks his former business partner, Alan Hollingsworth. Gray declares that Alan has swindled villagers who have invested in his plans for a crafts centre at the nearby mill. Concerned locals respond by setting up an action group to recover their cash, headed by pompous local publican Nigel Anderson and his edgy wife, Doreen. Barnaby learns that his old friends, George and Catherine Bullard, have also been investors and that Catherine, a local councillor, was once threatened by Gray over a planning issue concerning the mill. Alan's temptress wife, Simone, then disappears, and a kidnap is suspected, but, when a murder ensues, Barnaby and Troy have a multi-layered investigation on their hands. It is not long before Barnaby has discovered that everyone has a secret to hide, even faded actress Elfrida Molfrey and her doddery companion, Bunny Dawlish. Reg Buckley, company secretary of the mill enterprise, appears to have rather expensive tastes for his modest income; his wife, Felicity, seems notably remote from her family, and their daughter, Brenda, has a secret obsession. Who is the mysterious Harry Vellacott who calls to see Alan, and why is village potter Sarah Lawton attending the action group meetings when she has never invested in the mill? For Barnaby, Morton Fendle is not so much an idyllic English village as a 'cess pit' that urgently needs cleansing.

Gray Patterson (Mark Bazeley) takes cover behind Sarah Lawton (Tessa Peake-Jones).

Tessa Peake-Jones (Sarah Lawton)

'Where's Del Boy?', is the common question shouted at Tessa Peake-Jones when she goes shopping, referring, of course, to her high profile role as Raquel in the magnificent BBC comedy *Only Fools and Horses*. Series as triumphant as that tend to overshadow an actor's other work, which in Tessa's case is far from insignificant. Early appearances came in *Telford's Change*, *Pride and Prejudice* and *Up the Garden Path*, with other credits following in series such as *The Demon Headmaster* and *Tom Jones*. On joining the *Midsomer* crew as gullible potter Sarah Lawton, Tessa at least knew one member of the cast extremely well. Laura Howard (Cully) had previously played Tessa's daughter in the ghostly sitcom, *So Haunt Me*.

Michele Dotrice (Felicity Buckley)

It's taken Michele Dotrice years to escape from the shadow of Betty, the long-suffering wife of Frank Spencer (Michael Crawford), the character she played in *Some Mothers Do 'Ave 'Em* – this despite a host of credits in such programmes as *A Month in the Country*, *Chintz*, *Boon*, *The Winslow Boy*, *Vanity Fair*, *Give Us a Clue* and *Bramwell*, plus Shakespearean drama. The part of the icy Felicity Buckley in 'Faithful Unto Death', however, certainly helped Michele shrug off Betty's good-natured innocence once and for all. Daughter of Roy Dotrice and sister

Above left:
Michele
Dotrice as
Felicity
Buckley.

Above right:
Doreen and
Nigel
Anderson
(Rosalind
Ayres and
Paul Brooke)
at the village
fête.

of Karen Dotrice, Michele is married to Edward Woodward, with whom she once appeared in *The Equaliser*.

Peter Jones (Bunny Dawlish)

The late Peter Jones was a familiar face in British TV comedy for four decades, making his mark initially as harassed factory boss Mr Fenner in *The Rag Trade*. He followed this up with starring roles in sitcoms such as *Beggar My Neighbour* and *Mr Digby, Darling*, contributing later to successes such as *The Goodies*, *Whoops Apocalypse* and *The Hitch-Hiker's Guide to the Galaxy*. Peter was also a popular choice for parts in straight(er) dramas and these included *C.A.T.S. Eyes*, *Rumpole of the Bailey* and *Holby City*. To his 'Faithful Unto Death' character of Bunny Dawlish, Peter typically brought a dash of light humour, gentle relief from the dark deeds that threaten to swamp Morton Fendle. He died in 2000.

'Faithful Unto Death' is the first episode in which Troy does not wear a wedding ring. Indeed, he openly declares himself to be a single man early in the episode.

Death in Disguise

Cast

Guy Gamelin	Miles Anderson
Trixie Channing . .	Tilly Blackwood
Suhami/Sylvie Gamelin .	Anna Bolt
Heather Beavers	Diane Bull
May Cuttle	Judy Cornwell
Ken Beavers	Colin Farrell
Ian Craigie	Michael Feast
Tim Riley	Daniel Hart
Arno Gibbs	Charles Kay
Christopher Wainwright . .	Stephen Moyer
William Carter .	Robert Pickavance
Felicity Gamelin	Susan Tracy
Ava Rokeby	Dolly Wells
Terry Lightfoot	Ashley Artus
Mrs Cook	Mary Healey
Raymond Jennings .	Graham Turner
Researcher	Caroline Lintott
Interviewer	Jon Glover
Newscaster	Geoffrey Beevers
Waitress	Siobhan O'Carroll

Credits

Writer	Douglas Watkinson
Novel	Caroline Graham
Producers	Betty Willingale, Brian True-May
Director	Baz Taylor
Transmitted . . .	Wednesday, 6 May 1998, 8–10pm ITV

Story line

Previous page: May the sun shine: celestial light falls on May Cuttle (Judy Cornwell).

The serenity of life at The Lodge of the Golden Windhorse is about to be shattered. When co-founder Bill Carter falls to his death, a tragic accident is presumed, but perceptions change when a giant stone cannonball falls from the roof during a storm and nearly kills the commune's mother figure, May Cuttle. However, it is with the murder of the Lodge's revered Master, Ian Craigie, that Causton CID really begins to take an interest. Barnaby and Troy launch themselves into a tricky investigation involving complex personal relationships and murky pasts, hindered at every turn by the suspects' New Age fascination with the afterlife and the power of cosmic energy. Hippyish couple Ken and Heather Beavers are particularly irritating, former legal clerk Arno Gibbs seems deliberately evasive and new arrival Christopher Wainwright is not what he claims to be. His girlfriend, Suhami, has fled from the boorishness of her unscrupulous businessman father, Guy Gamelin, and her alcoholic, drug-dependent mother, Felicity, but both have followed her to the

An edited down, 90-minute version of 'Death in Disguise' was shown as a repeat by ITV on 18 August 2000.

Lodge for her eighteenth birthday dinner. Strangely detached from the other-worldliness of her fellow interns is prickly Trixie Channing, and completing the wacky household is Tim Riley, a manic, shy boy whose painful past has turned him into a frightened mute. With the local press snooping around, Barnaby needs a convincing result before the story breaks.

Judy Cornwell (May Cuttle)

Splendidly re-creating the flouncy, bouncy, over-the-top enthusiasm of Golden Windhorse matriarch May Cuttle, Judy Cornwell arrived in *Midsomer* after years of prime-time appearances. She received a nomination for a BAFTA award in the 1970s for her role as Rosie in *Cakes and Ale* and also starred in such dramas as *Mill on the Floss*, *Jane Eyre* and *Persuasion*, plus lighter fare such as *Boon*, *Miss Marple*, *Rumpole of the Bailey*, *Bergerac*, *The Bill*, *There Comes a Time...* and *Moody and Pegg*. To many viewers, she is best known, however, as Daisy in the Roy Clarke comedy *Keeping Up Appearances*.

It's all New Age nonsense to Barnaby.

Death's Shadow

Story line

Inspector Barnaby finds himself once more in the quirky village of Badger's Drift. This time it is for happier reasons – he thinks. Joyce has decided that, as a silver wedding anniversary treat, she and her husband will renew their wedding vows, and Tom has suggested the attractive, old church of St Michael's, which he visited when investigating the bizarre goings on a couple of years earlier. Genial vicar Stephen Wentworth welcomes the Barnabys with open arms but, as the great day approaches, a brutal murder scatters the best-laid plans to the wind. The victim is local property developer Richard Bayly, a man who

*Above:
Gordon
Gostelow
adds another
string to his
bow as
villager
Reginald
Williams.*

has just been diagnosed as suffering from a malignant brain tumour. He has made plenty of enemies thanks to his insensitive building plans in the village, including his former head teacher Agnes Sampson and two former school friends, estate worker David Whitely and estate agent Ian Eastman. But who would be vicious enough to slay him with an ornamental Indian sword? Could the vicar's disdainful wife, who has little time for any of the villagers, have wielded the blade? Or the Williamses, Agnes's sister and brother-in-law, who once ran the post office and are stalwarts of village life? Did Bayly's doctor, Barbara Henson, have a motive, and was the return to the area of Simon Fletcher, a local boy made good in the theatre, of any significance? And what secret is teenager Charles Jennings keen to hide? Barnaby has much to resolve before he can offer Joyce the joyous wedding anniversary she so richly deserves.

*Opposite:
A convincing
cleric:
Richard
Briers as
Stephen
Wentworth.*

'I don't think I've ever had a happier television experience than when I was working with Betty Willingale and Jeremy Silberston,' recalls writer Anthony Horowitz. 'There was just total devotion to what we were doing. You can glimpse me in 'Death's Shadow', next to Betty, singing in the church. That day was such a happy day. We had fits of giggles about some terrible joke made by Nick Dunning, who played estate agent Ian Eastman. It's rare to be in a television show these days where you can have such fun.'

'I have had the worst line in the series', laughs Daniel Casey, referring to a scene in 'Death's Shadow'. On inspecting one of the victims, the script called for Troy to ask: 'What's that he's got in his hand?', only for Bullard to reply: 'It's a pear.' 'I argued long and hard that I didn't want to say that line,' says Daniel, 'because you'd have to be desperately dense not to be able to recognize that someone's holding a pear. But it stayed in.'

Richard Briers (Stephen Wentworth)

Actor Simon Fletcher (Julian Wadham) opens Badger's Drift's fateful fête.

Playing a vicar was nothing new to Richard Briers, one of the biggest names to guest star in *Midsomer Murders*. In the 1980s he spent three years in the cloth as Reverend Philip Lambe in the sitcom *All in Good Faith*. 'I always look very convincing and reckon I could have been a vicar,' he says. 'It's partly my face and having a rather big nose, I think.' However, Richard is still fondly remembered by most viewers as the genially self-sufficient Tom Good from the 1970s sitcom *The Good Life*, even though there are numerous other roles that have endeared Briers to the British nation. These include pedantic busybody Martin Bryce in *Ever Decreasing Circles*, the Walter Mitty-like Ralph Tanner in *The Other One*, over-optimistic journalist Travis Kent in *Goodbye Mr Kent* and eccentric Hector Macdonald, laird of Glenbogle, in *Monarch of the Glen*. These came after early starring roles in the comedies *Brothers in Law*, *Marriage Lines* and *Ben Travers Farces*. His distinctive, whimsical voice has characterized such popular animations as *Roobarb* and *Noah and Nelly*, but, in contrast, there has been acclaim for his notable Shakespearean work, too.

Cast

Stephen Wentworth	Richard Briers
Claire Williams	Anna Cropper
Ian Eastman	Nick Dunning
Reginald Williams	Gordon Gostelow
Richard Bayly	Dominic Jephcott
Angela Wentworth	Judy Parfitt
Agnes Sampson	Vivian Pickles
Dr Barbara Henson	Mossie Smith
Brenda Eastman	Jessica Turner
David Whitely	Christopher Villiers
Simon Fletcher	Julian Wadham
Charles Jennings	Terence Corrigan
Olive Beauvoisin	Eileen Davies
Mr Jocelyne	Timothy Bateson
Mrs Bundy	Marlene Sidaway
PC Angel	Neil Conrich
Felix Bryce	Nick Robinson

Credits

Writer	Anthony Horowitz
Producers	Betty Willingale, Brian True-May
Director	Jeremy Silberston
Transmitted	Wednesday, 20 January 1999, 8–10pm ITV

Strangler's Wood

Story line

The discovery of the naked body of a young woman in Raven's Wood brings back distressing memories for the inhabitants of a quiet Midsomer village. She has been strangled with a necktie. Nine years earlier, three other such deaths were discovered, since when this tract of wilderness has been nicknamed 'Strangler's Wood'. As Barnaby and Troy begin their investigation they are plagued with advice from George Meakham, the detective who failed to catch the killer all those years ago. Meakham is now so obsessed with his failure that he has retired into the village with his wife, Emily, and finds it hard to stay away from the woods. He is convinced the same killer is on the loose but Barnaby is more cautious. For Barnaby the question is not so much why the killings have started again as why they stopped in the first place. The identity of the latest victim is established as Carla Constanza, a model who was the face of Carla cigarettes in Brazil. She had booked into a local hotel, run by repellent Leonard Pike and his reclusive, terminally ill mother, but had barely used her room. On the day of her death, her diary flags up an appointment with a mysterious person named Draycott. Based in the same village is Monarch Tobacco, the company that manufactures the cigarette brand, so suspicion falls on its executives, especially managing director Bill Mitchell and marketing director John Merrill. But, as Bill protests, why would the company want to kill off the woman whose image was central to the success of the brand? John seems a more likely suspect. He has been using the same hotel for secret liaisons with divorcée Liz Frances, with whom his wife, Kate, writes an agony aunt column for the local rag. More relevantly, there is an abundance of evidence to place him at the crime scene. Yet, Barnaby thinks, the Merrills' schoolboy son, David, and Portuguese au pair, Anna Santarosa, are also behaving suspiciously. Meanwhile, in London, a Harley Street doctor's surgery is set ablaze, with the body of a man inside. With Joyce away tending to her sick mother, it is Cully who on this occasion bears the brunt of disrupted mealtimes and social evenings as Barnaby's detective mind is preoccupied with finding the murderer.

Opposite: A game of bowls provides little respite for George Markham (Frank Windsor).

Below: David Merrill (Tom Eilenberg) spies on Barnaby and Troy.

Frank Windsor (George Meakham)

'Strangler's Wood' provided an opportunity for a 'marital' reunion between Frank Windsor and Anne Stallybrass. The experienced duo had previously headlined as a husband and wife in Yorkshire Television's *Flying Lady*, a light drama about a Rolls-Royce hire service. It is intriguing that in 'Strangler's Wood' Frank plays a retired policeman, haunted by an unsolved crime, because, of course, his major television claim to fame was as John Watt, the detective star of *Z Cars*, *Softly Softly* and *Second Verdict*. As the gentler foil for the blustering Charlie Barlow, played by the late Stratford Johns, it was a role that Frank played, off and on, for 14 years. Title roles in later dramas such as *The Real Eddy English* and *Headmaster* were accompanied by parts in series such as *September Song*, *Anchor Me*, *Kidnapped*, *Into the Labyrinth*, *Boon* and *Peak Practice*.

Cast

Dorothea Pike	Kathleen Byron
Anna Santarosa	Debbie Chazen
Bill Mitchell	Jeremy Clyde
David Merrill	Tom Eilenberg
Leonard Pike	Peter Eyre
John Merrill	Nick Farrell
Kate Merrill	Phyllis Logan
Carla Constanza	Betti Romani
Emily Meakham	Anne Stallybrass
Liz Frances	Trudie Styler
George Meakham	Frank Windsor
Dan Peterson	Toby Jones
Sebastian Renwick	Cyril Shaps
Gloria Bradley	Katy Brittain
PC Angel	Neil Conrich
Nick	Frankie Carson
Milkman	Anthony Howes
Ticket seller	Elizabeth Tyrrell
Ad woman	Tara Hugo
Brazilian bandit	George Lane Cooper
Path lab assistant	Rebecca Charles

Credits

Writer	Anthony Horowitz
Producers	Betty Willingale, Brian True-May
Director	Jeremy Silberston
Transmitted	Wednesday, 3 February 1999, 8–10pm ITV

Phyllis Logan (Kate Merrill)

Love and Reason, *Kavanagh QC*, *Invasion Earth*, *All the King's Men*, *Heartbeat* and *Inspector Morse* are just a handful of the dramas in which Phyllis Logan has appeared, with the role of consultant cardiologist Muriel McKendrick in *Holby City* one of her most recent successes. However, it is as Lovejoy's posh associate, Lady Jane Felsham, that she is probably best recalled by most viewers. It was often intimated that Lady Jane would eventually trip up the aisle with the roguish antiques dealer played by Ian McShane, but it

never actually happened. In 'Strangler's Wood', Phyllis plays a worried wife who perhaps wishes she'd had been as clear-headed as Lady Jane and steered clear of marriage, too.

Above: An agony aunt with problems of her own: Kate Merrill (Phyllis Logan) no longer trusts her husband, John.

Left: Barnaby and Troy struggle to see the wood for the trees.

Dead Man's Eleven

Story line

Summer in Midsomer would not be complete without cricket on the village green. The village on this occasion is Fletcher's Cross, just one of the rural communities earmarked by Joyce as a possible retirement home for her and Tom, now that Cully has moved to London with Nico. As the evocative thwack of willow on leather resounds in the distance, the Barnabys begin their house-hunt, immediately encountering Colin and Christine Cooper, a strangely sheepish pair of born-again Christians who seem to have greater resources than their modest employments would supply. With the DCI's nostrils twitching with suspicion, the scene is set for the unearthing of yet more dark village secrets, secrets that begin to out with the murder – by cricket bat – of the young wife of the local squire, Robert Cavendish. Robert is a deeply unpopular man, a selfish tycoon who has made his fortune in quarrying stone and throws his weight around with the same delicacy. When his financially embarrassed son, Stephen, becomes chief suspect for murder number two – in the cricket scorebox – and a whiff of blackmail sours the summer air, the Barnaby brow becomes even more furrowed. Stephen has been having an affair with barmaid Tricia Smith and his lonely wife, Jane, is clearly unhappy with her lot, which puts her firmly in the frame. There is also Iain Frasier, a disgruntled former Cavendish employee, to consider, plus his rambler wife, Zelda, who is fighting vainly to re-open a footpath across the Cavendishes' land. Mrs Wilson, the Cavendish housekeeper, is always conveniently close to events, while elderly Doreen Beavis, who lives next to the cricket field, is surely cannier than her dippy exterior suggests. With Troy – opening the batting for rivals Midsomer Worthy – well-placed to pick up gossip, Barnaby is hopeful that this case will not leave him 'stumped' for long.

Robert Hardy (Robert Cavendish)

By the time Robert Hardy paid a visit to *Midsomer*, he'd had plenty of experience in playing truculent bosses and hard-headed men, which made him a perfect choice for the part of the unscrupulous Robert Cavendish. Roles such as Alec Stewart in *The Troubleshooters*, Twiggy Rathbone in *Hot Metal*, Sergeant Gratz in *Manhunt* and Sir Herbert Hamilton in *Bramwell* come to mind, along with the more genial creation of vet Siegfried Farnon in *All Creatures Great and Small*.

Opposite: Backward point? Barnaby and Troy discover murder in the scorebox.

Truculent and hard-headed: Robert Cavendish (Robert Hardy) is a bad loser.

Annabelle Apsion (Jane Cavendish)

Chiefly known for a number of years as widow Joy Wilton in *Soldier, Soldier*, Annabelle Apsion's career took a darker turn when she was cast as the devious Beverly in Jimmy McGovern's *The Lakes*. It was a similar quirky mysteriousness that she brought to 'Dead Man's Eleven' as Jane, the betrayed wife of Stephen Cavendish, moping around in the background, greedily snatching whatever food was on offer, but hinting to the viewer that she was capable of considerably more sinful deeds. Among her other major credits have been *Big Women*, *My Good Friend*, *Sunburn*, *Micawber* and the award-winning dramas *Hillsborough* and *Goodnight Mister Tom*.

Duncan Preston (Colin Cooper)

'It was good to do something less comic.' That was the view of Duncan Preston, who is undoubtedly better known for his humorous performances. These have included roles as anaesthetist Jonathan Haslam in *Surgical Spirit*, Kevin the teenager's dad in *Harry Enfield and Chums*, and in many parts alongside Victoria Wood (particularly as Stan in *dinnerladies*). In *Midsomer Murders* Duncan proved that he could turn a more sinister face to the audience. There is plenty of humour in his kinky on-screen relationship with Imelda Staunton, but Duncan's character, Colin Cooper, displays a guilty edginess that belies his genial facade. The acting even continued on the cricket pitch. Colin Cooper, like the others, was meant to be a shambling amateur but Duncan was actually a very good player when young. 'It's difficult to play absolutely badly if you can play a bit,' he commented when making the episode, recalling how he used to practise with Yorkshire when a teenager.

The sporting side of Gavin Troy comes to the fore in 'Dead Man's Eleven'. He has responded to an advert asking for players for Midsomer Worthy's cricket team and proves to be a useful acquisition for the side. But, while actor Daniel Casey has always followed cricket, he'd never really played before and concedes he had to learn from scratch.

Imelda Staunton (Christine Cooper)

Like Duncan Preston, Imelda Staunton can play it straight or for laughs, which is just as well when a juicy role like Christine Cooper is offered. 'The draw of the job is that she is a bit off-centre and not Mrs Ordinary,' Imelda remarked. 'Christine and Colin are living a lie. I love the fact that on the surface they're middle England but scratch that surface and there's something a bit weird going on, to do with religion and sex.' Shortly after filming *Midsomer Murders*, Imelda starred as Mrs Micawber in the BBC's *David Copperfield*, a role later filled by her 'Dead Man's Eleven' co-star Annabelle Apsion in ITV's *Micawber*. Among Imelda's other TV credits have been the sitcoms *Up The Garden Path*, *If You See God*, *Tell Him* and *Is It Legal?*.

Cast

Jane Cavendish	Annabelle Apsion
Mrs Wilson	Penelope Beaumont
Doreen Beavis	Hilda Braid
Stephen Cavendish	Anthony Calf
Tara Cavendish	Felicity Dean
Robert Cavendish	Robert Hardy
Patricia Smith	Zoë Hart
Zelda Frasier	Delia Lindsay
Colin Cooper	Duncan Preston
Ian Frasier	Terence Rigby
Christine Cooper	Imelda Staunton
Emily Beavis	Susan Field
Charles Jennings	Terence Corrigan
Dan Peterson	Toby Jones
Olive Beauvoisin	Eileen Davies
Matthew Draper	Joss Gower
Young Trish	Ella Jones
Rambler (Edwina)	Amanda Walker

Credits

Writer	Anthony Horowitz
Producer	Betty Willingale
Executive Producer	Brian True-May
Director	Jeremy Silberston
Transmitted	Sunday, 12 September 1999, 8.30–10.30pm ITV

Blood Will Out

Story line

The village of Martyr Warren is on the brink of turmoil. A well-known traveller, Orville Tudway, has returned in his gypsy caravan and is planning a get-together of other roving folk. This does not go down well with local magistrate Hector Bridges, or local farmer Tilly Dinsdale, who fear their livestock will be rustled. Barnaby is called in to restore calm. He declares that the travellers have committed no crime and can stay, but warns them to be on their best behaviour. Determined to move them on, Hector calls up some of his old army pals during the night. Barnaby, acting on an anonymous tip-off, arrives in time to prevent bloodshed. However, soon afterwards, the travellers stage a frenetic pony-and-trap race, after which Hector is found murdered and a silver wine cooler stolen from his house. Finding the killer is not going to be easy, as there are many suspicious candidates. Hector's wife, Jenny, has clearly fallen out of love with him; his teenage daughter, Fleur, seems only concerned with his money; local shop assistant Stefan Miller has sworn revenge after being jailed by Hector, and his boss, Peter Fairfax, also turns out to have had good reason for wanting Hector dead. Peter's lady friend, Tilly's sister Felicity, remains remarkably calm about the whole business, in contrast to nervous Will and Muriel Saxby, who have close but baffling connections with the Bridges' household. Then there are the travellers to consider, particularly Orville, who shares an army past with Hector and is clearly troubled by a letter he has just received, and the petty-thieving Smith clan, headed by granddad John, and brother and sister Michael and Rachel. For Barnaby, the case at least provides a diversion from the torment of the rigid diet Joyce and Cully have devised for him, a regime Troy is charged with enforcing.

Above: Under suspicion: Michael and John Smith (Nick Moran and Jerome Willis).

Opposite: Almost as colourful as his van: trouble travels with Orville Tudway (Kevin McNally).

Phyllida Law (Felicity Dinsdale)

For former Play School presenter Phyllida Law, the attraction of a part in *Midsomer Murders* lay in the deliberate absence of sensationalism. 'It's the sort of programme I love to watch,' she admitted. 'I'm glad it's not full of sex and violence because that makes me run into the hall screaming.' Law, who married the late Eric Thompson, voice of *The Magic Roundabout* in the 1960s, is well-known as the mother of actresses Emma and Sophie Thompson but has a wonderfully long career to her own name, with appearances in *About Face, Ffizz, Hell's Bells, That's Love, Wonderful You, Stig of the Dump* and *The Swap* among other series.

Kevin McNally
(Orville Tudway)

A secret to hide? Edgy Will and Muriel Saxby (John Duttine and Elizabeth Garvie).

'Orville's almost as colourful as his van,' said actor Kevin McNally about his travelling character in 'Blood Will Out'. 'He was hippyish but quite straight because of his past. I've played soldiers and hippies before but never at the same time. I'm a bit more the hippy – I like wandering about in the country.' Kevin's own career has also been colourful, wandering between drama and comedy in programmes as varied as *Crown Court*, *I, Claudius*, *Poldark*, *Diana*, *We'll Meet Again*, *Tygo Road*, *Frontiers*, *Underworld*, *Dad*, *Murder Most Horrid* and *Uprising*.

Cast

Stefan Miller	Daniel Betts
Tilly Dinsdale	Rowena Cooper
Will Saxby	John Duttine
Muriel Saxby	Elizabeth Garvie
Jenny Bridges	Tricia George
Hector Bridges	Paul Jesson
Felicity Dinsdale	Phyllida Law
Orville Tudway	Kevin McNally
Michael Smith	Nick Moran
Rachel Smith	Elizabeth Thomas
Peter Fairfax	Ian Thompson
Fleur Bridges	Honeysuckle Weeks
John Smith	Jerome Willis
Major Harry Tomkinson	David Allister
Shop assistant	Francis Lee

Credits

Writer	Douglas Watkinson
Producers	Betty Willingale, Brian True-May
Director	Moira Armstrong
Transmitted	Sunday, 19 September 1999, 9–11pm ITV

Death of a Stranger

Story line

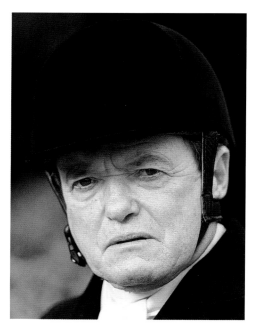

The Barnabys are on holiday in France but even over a relaxing dinner in a gourmet restaurant the sound of murder is never far from Tom's ears. James Fitzroy, a pompous old acquaintance, who is on a hunting trip, can't resist reporting that a tramp has been killed back in his home village of Marshwood. He says that Barnaby's locum, Superintendent Ron Pringle, who is retiring into the village, has already found the culprit. Knowing Pringle's prejudices, Barnaby can't help thinking that such a swift conclusion to the case is a matter of concern. On his return to Causton, he and Troy survey the scene. The tramp has been seen in the village only recently. He has been bothering Linda Wagstaff, a reclusive, theatrical woman who lives in a converted railway carriage in the woods where the tramp's body was found. The land belongs to Grahame Tranter, who inherited it from his father, who went missing 30 years before and had been officially declared dead. Grahame's mother, Marcia, is joint master of foxhounds (with James Fitzroy) of the village hunt. Mercilessly overbearing, she has never seen eye-to-eye with Grahame's townie wife, Kate, yet Kate, for her own part, seems happier away from her husband than alongside him. Pringle has arrested local tearaway Billy Gurdie for the murder, but the plot thickens when Billy's father is murdered, again in the woods. Amid 'Tally Ho' scenes of hunting activity, Barnaby tries to untangle the personal relationships that seem to lie at the heart of these baffling murders and attempts to identify a 'headless' woman seen in compromising pictures found near the tramp's den. Drawing into his enquiries a weasely taxidermist named Henry Carstairs (who also has claims on the land), Billy's friend Dave Hedges and Sarah Fitzroy, James's downtrodden wife, Barnaby sets out to outfox his quarries and hound them into submission.

James Bolam (Ron Pringle)

James Bolam admits to never having watched an episode of *Midsomer Murders* before he accepted the role of Ron Pringle, the retiring policeman who aspires to join the local hunt. 'The role appealed to me because of the character and the riding,' he said. 'I used to ride years ago but I don't do it at all now, so it was a very jolly job.' The part of the proud, snobby Pringle is a long way removed from Bolam's best known TV creations, the bolshie Terry Collier in *The Likely Lads* and union militant Jack Ford in *When the Boat Comes In*, in fact quite different to most roles he has undertaken in his long career. These have included starring parts in series such as *The Beiderbecke Affair*, *Only When I Laugh*, *Second Thoughts*, *The Stalker's Apprentice*, *The Missing Postman*, *Room at the Bottom*, *Father Matthew's Daughter*, *Andy Capp*, *Dirty Tricks*, *Close and True* and *Pay and Display*.

Cast

Ron Pringle	James Bolam
Betty Pringle	Janet Dale
Marcia Tranter	Diane Fletcher
Linda Wagstaff	Jeanne Hepple
Sarah Fitzroy	Jennifer Hilary
James Fitzroy	Richard Johnson
Henry Carstairs	Simon McBurney
Grahame Tranter	Dominic Mafham
Ben Gurdie	Fred Ridgeway
Billy Gurdie	Tom Smith
Cathy Gurdie	Jane Wood
Kate Tranter	Sarah Winman
Tramp	Peter Bayliss
Dan Peterson	Toby Jones
Dave Hedges	Jonie Broom
Sandra	Patricia Valentine
Charlotte	Arlene Cockburn
Policeman	David Maybrick
Matron	Shenagh Govan
Fred Rodale	Frank Mills
Lady Bracknell	Eve Pearce
Jack Worthing	Grant Gillespie
Director	Simon Greiff

Credits

Writer	Douglas Watkinson
Executive Producer	Brian True-May
Producer	Peter Cregeen
Director	Peter Cregeen
Transmitted	Friday, 31 December 1999, 9–10.55pm ITV

Richard Johnson (James Fitzroy)

Greatly respected actor Richard Johnson had mixed thoughts on being offered a return to hunting in 'Death of a Stranger'. 'I used to chase foxes, I'm slightly ashamed to say now,' he recalls. 'In a civilized society we shouldn't really be doing this for fun. It just doesn't wash any more. When we were out filming *Midsomer Murders* with the horses and hounds I saw again the thrill and the enjoyment of it. I just don't think it should be at the expense of another animal.' Richard's career extends over half a century. He has worked alongside greats like John Geilgud and with the RSC. On television, his best-known roles have been in dramas such as *Supply and Demand*, *Breaking the Code*, *Murder She Wrote*, *Treasure Island*, *P.G. Wodehouse's Heavy Weather* and *The Camomile Lawn*.

Left: Woodland prowler–taxidermist Henry Carstairs (Simon McBurney) searches for bodies.

Below: Who is Linda Wagstaff's (Jeanne Hepple) secret long-lost lover?

Blue Herrings

Cast

Madge Fielding	Georgine Anderson
Arthur Prewitt	Geoffrey Bayldon
Cyril Toft	Sam Beazley
Alice Bly	Phyllis Calvert
William Smithers	Nigel Davenport
Pru Bennett	Angela Down
Hilary Richards	Deborah Findlay
Muriel Harrap	Matyelok Gibbs
Nurse O'Casey	Mali Harries
Nurse Bartlett	Miranda Kingsley
Sister Lovelace	Carolyn Pickles
Mungo Mortimer	Colin Tierney
Celia Armstrong	Gudrun Ure
Marjorie 'George' Watson	Mary Wimbush
Dr Clive Warnford	Clive Wood
Miss Laybourne	Daphne Goddard
Landlord	Arthur Cox
Jeweller	Cyril Shaps
Florist	Caroline John
Shop assistant	Sarah Ball
Hotel receptionist	Katherine Tozer
Waiter	David Killick

Credits

Writer	Hugh Whitemore
Executive Producer	Brian True-May
Producer	Peter Cregeen
Director	Peter Smith
Transmitted	Saturday, 22 January 2000, 8.55–10.50pm ITV

Story line

Previous page: 'I'm listening'... Tom tries to reassure his worried Auntie Alice (Phyllis Calvert) ...

It's a fresh start for the Barnabys in their new home. Tom has taken a week off work to decorate but first visits his Auntie Alice, who has taken up temporary residence in the Lawnside private nursing home near Aspern Tallow. She is clearly distressed, however, and tells her nephew that elderly resident Muriel Harrap has died unexpectedly in the night. The attendant doctor, Clive Warnford, has diagnosed a heart attack but she has it on good authority from fellow inmate 'George' Watson that the deceased – not a popular person – had recently been given the all clear by a specialist. Rumour has it that Dr Warnford and the home's manager, Hilary Richards, are swindling clients by making them change their wills. Barnaby visits the unco-operative Dr Warnford, admires his Aston Martin and notices that he seems to be rather better off than a rural doctor would normally be. Further deaths among the Lawnside residents continue to unnerve Alice. Barnaby tries to reassure her and dispatches Troy to make some enquiries among the guests. The sergeant is struck by the obvious air of guilt hovering around former teacher Arthur Prewitt, but gets on famously with the other residents, including roguish old bounder William Smithers. Troy also hears of the suspicious movements of car dealer Mungo Mortimer, whose mother had died at Lawnside a few weeks previously. Barnaby, meanwhile, expressing his condolences to Pru Bennett, niece of one of the deceased, finds her strangely jumpy and distracted. Now the decorating must wait as Tom works his way through what the confused 'George' describes as 'blue herrings' – a whole ocean of them – in order to restore calm at Lawnside.

Phyllis Calvert (Alice Bly)

After a film and television career that had spanned six decades, 83-year-old Phyllis Calvert was coaxed out of retirement to take the part of Barnaby's favourite aunt, Alice Bly, in 'Blue Herrings'. 'I retired about eight years ago,' she said at the time, 'but when this job came up I did it because I thought it would be rather fun.' She did notice a few changes on set, however. 'In my day we did most things in the studio whereas now they do it all over the place and you spend your days in a caravan.' Among Phyllis's best-known films are *Kipps*, *Fanny By Gaslight*, *Mandy* and *Oh, What a Lovely War*; on television she starred in the 1971 series *Kate*, playing *Heart and Home* magazine agony aunt Kate Graham. Other credits have come in such series as *After Henry*, *Victoria Wood* and *The House of Eliott*.

... but there's plenty to trouble her at Lawnside.

Geoffrey Bayldon (Arthur Prewitt)

The filming of *Midsomer Murders* is often seen as an actors' reunion, as Geoffrey Bayldon discovered on accepting the part of fastidious pensioner Arthur Prewitt. 'I began my professional acting career on the same day as Mary Wimbush (George Watson), after her brother-in-law, who was my entertainments officer in the RAF, suggested I went for an audition with the BBC,' he remembers. 'I also did a serial called *All Passion Spent* with Phyllis Calvert. Then, of course, I worked with John Nettles in *Bergerac*. It was great to be back with them all again.' Geoffrey is, however, undoubtedly best remembered as the 11th-century wizard, Catweazle, in the 1970s children's series of the same name – this despite the fact that he has been seen in scores of major programmes over the years, including *Devenish*, *Blott on the Landscape*, *Hold the Back Page*, *The Prince and the Pauper*, *Peak Practice*, *Casualty*, *Worzel Gummidge* and *Fort Boyard*.

There's more to William Smithers (Nigel Davenport) than meets the eye.

Gudrun Ure (Celia Armstrong)

Like Geoffrey Bayldon, Gudrun Ure is fondly remembered for a supernatural children's TV creation. In Gudrun's case, it is 1980s heroine *Supergran*, who, endowed with unusual powers after being struck by a magic ray, mounted her famous 'flycycle' to defend the good citizens of Chisleton. Her role in 'Blue Herrings' is noticeably more sedate, her character, Celia Armstrong, suffering from a terminal illness, but Gudrun was not concerned about the sometimes depressing retirement home scenario. 'When you get to my age, it's something that is looking at us as an all too realistic possibility, so I wasn't frightened at the prospect of playing a resident like Celia. We filmed in a lovely location, it was summer and the gardens were beautiful. It was super.' Viewers may also recall her performances in such comedies and dramas as *Life After Life*, *Second Thoughts*, *Moon and Son* and *The Crow Road*.

With Barnaby 'off-duty' for much of 'Blue Herrings', viewers gain an extra insight into his personal life – and in particular his casual dress sense. 'Previously he's always been in a three-piece suit,' said star John Nettles, 'and I'm afraid his taste is as appalling in its casual mode as it is in its formal mode. Dreadful jeans and bomber jackets.'

Nigel Davenport (William Smithers)

Ruthless businessmen and awkward old buffers have become almost stock in trade to Nigel Davenport, thanks to a long career that has taken in roles such as Jim Fraser in *Oil Strike North*, Sir Edward Frere in *Howards' Way* and James Brant in *Trainer*. His character in 'Blue Herrings', William Smithers, is another wily old fox with a glint in the eye that suggests he has a few secrets up his sleeve. Nigel, father of actors Jack, Hugo and Laura Davenport, has also featured prominently in such series as *South Riding*, *Don't Rock the Boat*, *Prince Regent*, *Bird of Prey* and *Longitude*.

Judgement Day

Story line

It's Joyce's turn to take the limelight for once when she wins a contest in *Country Matters* magazine to be a judge for its 'Perfect Village' competition. One of the finalists is Midsomer Mallow, near Causton, but things are far from perfect in this particular hamlet. A spate of burglaries has alarmed locals and although the culprits – womanizing tearaway Peter Drinkwater and frustrated butcher's son Jack Dorset – are soon identified, the gruesome murder of Peter (stabbed by a pitchfork) sends shockwaves through the population. Nevertheless, the village committee decides to press ahead with its competition entry, hoping to keep the trouble out of the headlines until Judgement Day, when the four judges descend on the community. Because of the contest, Barnaby needs to tread carefully in his investigations: he doesn't want Joyce to know about these dark goings-on in case it prejudices her views. However, when Judgement Day arrives, and one of the judges is poisoned, the troubles of Midsomer Mallow can remain a secret no longer. There are a number of possible killers in the frame for the murder of Peter Drinkwater – spurned lovers Laura Brierly and Caroline Devere, for instance, as well as Laura's vet husband, Gordon, and Caroline's anxious parents, Marcus

Opposite: Tom with a character Timothy West 'has met before'.

Below: Barnaby and Troy take tea with vet's wife Laura Brierly (Marsha Fitzalan).

and Bella. But, who killed the judge, and for what possible reason, are questions without obvious answers. Edward Allardice, whose property was the last to be burgled and who threatened to kill the thieves, is particularly intriguing, because he declares his wife has died but there is no death certificate on record. Lucky for Tom, then, that Cully, who is researching a book about the history of the Causton Playhouse, has made friends with the retired actor. And then there is Peter's aunt, Barbara Drinkwater, who conducts the village orchestra, and seems more concerned about letting down her musical protégés than respecting her nephew's shocking death. Once again, for poor Joyce, her day in the sun is tarnished by the brutal demands of her husband's profession.

Last Judgement? The 'Perfect Village' contest takes its toll on panel chair Rosemary Furman (Maggie Steed).

Timothy West (Marcus Devere)

Having adopted one of his wonderful 'country gent' characterizations, Timothy West admits that the role of village council chairman Marcus Devere was familiar territory for him. 'I would say he was a character I have met before, certainly,' he says. There is one thing that does intrigue him about *Midsomer Murders*, however: 'There is a murder in every village – and yet it doesn't affect house prices!' Timothy's appearance in the series came immediately before that

of his wife, Prunella Scales, in 'Beyond The Grave', but Prunella's episode was actually filmed before his, which was in production at the time of 1999 solar eclipse. 'Shooting had to stop because we had no light,' he explains. 'I will always remember where I was that day.' The part of Devere follows countless major television roles, with highlights including starring parts in *Edward the Seventh*, *The Edwardians*, *Brass*, *The Monocled Mutineer*, *Blore MP* and various Shakespearean plays.

Cast

Peter Drinkwater . . Orlando Bloom
Laura Brierly . . . . . Marsha Fitzalan
Jane Rochelle . . . . . . Shelagh Fraser
Bella Devere . . . . . Hannah Gordon
Frank Mannion . . . . Nickolas Grace
Gordon Brierly . . . . . Richard Hope
Barbara Drinkwater . Barbara Jefford
Jack Dorset . . . . Tobias Menzies
Rosemary Furman . . . Maggie Steed
Samantha Johnstone . . . . Josephine
Tewson
Ray Dorset . . . . Bill Thomas
Caroline Devere . . . . . Chloe Tucker
Edward Allardice . . . Moray Watson
Marcus Devere . . . . . Timothy West
Ruth Weston . . . . . . Caroline Faber

Michael Weston . . . Richard Trinder
Annabel Weston . . . . . Emily Canfor-
Dumas
Dan Peterson . . . . Toby Jones
Mrs Foster . . . . . . Marlene Sidaway
Dr Sellers . . . . Robert Goodale
Alderman . . . . Malcolm Rennie
Alex . . . . Dominic Childs
James . . . . Cassian Horowitz

Credits

Writer . . . . Anthony Horowitz
Executive Producer . Brian True-May
Producer . . . . Betty Willingale
Director . . . . Jeremy Silberston
Transmitted . . Saturday, 29 January
2000, 8.55–10.55pm ITV

Nickolas Grace (Frank Mannion)

Alan Titchmarsh was the target when Nickolas Grace created the character of TV gardener Frank Mannion, one of the 'Perfect Village' judges in 'Judgement Day'. Grace decided to poke gentle fun at his friend in the short clip that was shown of his gardening show. 'I have worked with Alan on his chat show for Pebble Mill and on *Call My Bluff*. For fun, I put a bit of Alan in the character and I hope he will recognize it and laugh,' he said at the time. Frank's other trait is his limpness, echoing Nickolas's famous portrayal of the outrageous Anthony Blanche in *Brideshead Revisited*. 'I like the fact that Frank was very butch in front of the cameras but in real life was quite camp, suddenly saying "whoopsadaisy" when filming on his show had finished.' Nickolas has also been seen in many other TV productions, from *Robin of Sherwood* as the Sheriff of Nottingham, to *Birds of a Feather*, as Dorien's husband, Marcus.

Tolkien fans will be intrigued to note that this episode, which features Orlando Bloom – soon to be famous for his role in Lord of the Rings *– as Peter Drinkwater, also includes a house named 'Lothlorian', after the elvish valley in the Middle Earth masterpiece. Deliberate or coincidence? The latter, says writer Anthony Horowitz.*

Hannah Gordon (Bella Devere)

Bella donna: Hannah Gordon as the serene Mrs Devere.

Now well-known for presenting the painting series *Watercolour Challenge*, which visits almost as many beautiful villages as *Midsomer Murders*, Hannah Gordon has been one of British television's most recognizable actresses for over 30 years. Among her major roles have been Virginia Bellamy in *Upstairs, Downstairs*, Suzy Bassett alongside John Alderton in *My Wife Next Door*, Sylvia Telford with Peter Barkworth in *Telford's Change*, and opposite Richard Briers and Peter Egan, respectively, in the sitcoms *Goodbye Mr Kent* and *Joint Account*. She also bravely featured in *The Morecambe and Wise Show*. *Hadleigh, David Copperfield, Great Expectations, Jonathan Creek, Middlemarch, Taggart* and *My Family and Other Animals* are some of Hannah's other major credits.

Beyond the Grave

Cast

Anne Quarritch . . . . . Patricia Brake
Sandra MacKillop . Cheryl Campbell
James Tate . . . . . . James Laurenson
Linda Marquis . . Sylvestra Le Touzel
Charles MacKillop . . . . David Robb
Eleanor Bunsall . . . . Prunella Scales
Marcus Lowrie . . . . . Charles Simon
Alan Bradford . . . Malcolm Sinclair
Ralph Bailey . . . . Roger Sloman
Nico Bentley . . . . Ed Waters
PC Kevin Angel . . . . . Neil Conrich
Dr Catherine Bullard . Alwyne Taylor
Vicar . . . . Chris Stanton

Credits

Writer . . . . Douglas Watkinson
Producers . . . . Betty Willingale,
Brian True-May
Director . . . . Moira Armstrong
Transmitted . . . . Saturday,
5 February 2000, 8.55–10.55pm ITV

Story line

Proof that Midsomer was a magnet for dark deeds long before the arrival of Inspector Barnaby is provided in this tale with a Civil War background. The village is Aspern Tallow, where Aspern Hall was once the home of prominent Royalist Jonathan Lowrie. He was killed following a local battle in 1644, but his spirit returns to haunt present-day villagers. Particularly troubled is Alan Bradford, curator of the museum now housed in Lowrie's house, who calls in local picture restorer Sandra MacKillop when a portrait of Lowrie is found slashed. Barnaby considers the vandalism and declares the case to be of little interest, until he finds a packet of smoked mackerel in the adjoining churchyard. Smelling something fishy, he orders Troy into action, supported on this occasion by Cully's actor boyfriend, Nico Bentley, who has just landed a part in a police soap opera and is shadowing the detective sergeant as research for his role. Immediately the team unearth Bradford's criminal past and are surprised at Sandra's unhinged behaviour. Her gradual recovery from the death of her husband a year before has recently taken a turn for the worse and she has begun a sharp descent into paranoia, hastened by hallucinations experienced while she restores the portrait. Sandra is comforted by her caring brother-in-law, Charles, bereavement counsellor Linda Marquis and local clairvoyant Eleanor Bunsall, but, when the tomb of Jonathan Lowrie is looted and one of his distant

Previous page: Will Causton CID need the help of clairvoyant Eleanor Bunsall (Prunella Scales) to solve a crime 'Beyond the Grave'?

descendants is murdered, Sandra is not the only villager to feel somewhat insecure. Dragged into the inquiry are museum trustee James Tate and his daily help, Anne Quarritch, with whom he plans to start a new life in the South of France. Barnaby, as ever, keeps his feet on the ground and refuses to believe that events have a basis in the supernatural. But could he – just for once – be proved wrong?

Regular viewers might have spotted that in this episode the Barnabys appear to have moved back to their old house. Once again, this was the result of ITV screening episodes out of sequence. 'Beyond the Grave' was actually recorded with the previous year's episodes but was held back one series.

Patricia Brake (Anne Quarritch)

For Patricia Brake it was an eventful road from squeaky London teenager to a middle-aged charwoman in the village of Aspern Tallow. The viewing public's earliest memory of Patricia is probably as Ingrid, the daughter of wily old lag Fletcher, in *Porridge* and its sequel, *Going Straight*. She also played Eth in the TV version of *The Glums*. By the time she

Alan Bradford (Malcolm Sinclair) reports a ghostly, but violent, encounter to Barnaby.

'Beyond the Grave' does not hold the happiest memories for Daniel Casey. 'For one scene, I had to spend a day down a hole in a graveyard,' he remembers. 'I was 6ft under and it was made by proper gravediggers. I don't know if it had been inhabited before.'

became *Midsomer Murders'* cleaner and barmaid Anne Quarritch, her career had also taken in such series as *Second Time Around*, *Troubles & Strife*, *2 Point 4 Children* and the short-lived Spanish soap opera, *Eldorado*, in which she played queen bee Gwen Lockhead.

Cheryl Campbell (Sandra MacKillop)

Like Sandra, her bewildered character in 'Beyond The Grave', Cheryl Campbell may well have entered the world of art, rather than taking to the stage. 'I would have liked very much to go to art school as well as drama school,' she revealed, 'but I didn't want to do six years of study. If I had done it, I would have been a sculptress. Maybe I will

Troubled widow Sandra MacKillop (Cheryl Campbell) in the care of her devoted brother-in-law Charles (David Robb).

at some stage.' If the artistic route had been chosen, viewers would have missed out on numerous notable performances, particularly as schoolmistress Eileen in Dennis Potter's *Pennies from Heaven* and roles in the dramas *Testament of Youth*, *Malice Aforethought*, *The Mill on the Floss*, *Wing and a Prayer* and *Bramwell*. As well as Tom Barnaby, detectives Morse, Sherlock Holmes, Reg Wexford, Jack Frost and Miss Marple have all benefited from having Campbell prominent in their TV casebooks. More recently, she featured as Lady Carbery in the acclaimed BBC production of Trollope's *The Way We Live Now*.

Prunella Scales (Eleanor Bunsall)

From *Marriage Lines* with Richard Briers to Tesco advertisements with Jane Horrocks, Prunella Scales has worked with the best in the business, including John Nettles, with whom she once appeared in *Bergerac*. Inevitably, however, viewers will still picture her alongside John Cleese, as the dragon-like Sybill in *Fawlty Towers*, this despite a list of starring roles that most actors could only envy. To name but a few, these include *A Question of Attribution* (in which she played Her Majesty The Queen), *The Rector's Wife*, *Breaking The Code*, *After Henry* and *Mapp and Lucia*. Her first scene in 'Beyond The Grave' sees her pedalling a tricycle through the village, not as simple an act as you might think, as Prunella points out. 'I got on, refused to do a dry run and rode straight into a bank. I tried it twice more, then the director and prop man tried and they drove straight into the bank as well. We had forgotten that the technique is to remain completely upright and just turn the wheel.' In her capacity as President of the Council for the Protection of Rural England, no doubt she approves of the way in which *Midsomer Murders* makes full use of the beauty of the English countryside.

Garden of Death

Story line

When wayward shots ring out one summer afternoon it is clear that all is not well in the village of Midsomer Deverell. Fortunately, Tom Barnaby is on hand to apprehend the culprit, Rodney Widger, a nervous man who is angry that his privacy has been disturbed by the hordes of tourists (Tom and Joyce among them) who have begun to visit the gardens of Inkpen Manor. The house is the ancestral home of the Inkpen family but they have only just reclaimed the property having been forced to sell it 25 years before. Behind the new commercialism is Elspeth Inkpen-Thomas, who lives in the house with her snooty mother, Naomi, and two daughters, Fliss and Hilary. Fliss is the archetypal spoilt brat, with stunning blonde looks and an idle nature. She is cruelly patronizing to the more industrious Hilary, who is dark and dowdy. An illegitimate child, Hilary has only been back in the family fold for two years and the identity of her father remains a close secret. Elspeth has plans for Inkpen Manor and brazenly dismisses village objections to the redevelopment of a much-loved memorial garden into a tearoom. Among the opponents is Augustus Deverell, another local blue blood, whose son, Richard, is a bishop, but refuses to dress the part on a daily basis. Particularly against it is botanist

Opposite: Murder in the garden: a new case for Barnaby and Troy.

Left: There's trouble brewing in the normally peaceful village of Midsomer Deverell.

Cast

Fliss Inkpen-Thomas.Sarah Alexander
Augustus Deverell . . . Anthony Bate
Desmond Cox . . . Raymond Bowers
Susan Millard . . . . . . .Anna Calder-
Marshall
Charles King . . . . . . .Tom Chadbon
Richard Deverell . . Simon Chandler
Jane Bennett . . . . Kate Duchene
Daniel Bolt . . . . Neil Dudgeon
Hilary Inkpen . . .Victoria Hamilton
Marie Widger . . . . Shirley King
Elspeth Inkpen-Thomas . . . . Belinda
Lang
Cynthia Bennett . . . . Valerie Minifie
Rodney Widger . . . . . . .David Ross
Gerald Bennett . . . .Frederick Treves
Naomi Inkpen . . . Margaret Tyzack
Michael . . . . .Dean Batchelor
Archie Craddock . . . Neville Phillips
Mary . . . . Katherine Stark
Dean . . . . Michael Tucek
Elaine . . . . Elaine Donnelly

Credits

Writer . . . . .Christopher Russell
Producer . . . . Brian True-May
Director . . . . Peter Smith
Transmitted . . . . .Sunday, 10
September 2000, 9.00–11.00pm ITV

Jane Bennett, who is back in the village to care for her ailing dad, Gerald, who had laid the garden and then sold the house back to the Inkpens. A heated meeting in the village hall results in various people storming out early, which means there are plenty of suspects when Fliss is discovered murdered – beaten by a spade – in the disputed plot of land. Other figures in the frame include lecherous gardener Daniel Bolt, Rodney Widger's friend Charles King, shopkeeper Desmond Cox, and Susan Millard, wife of the local vicar, a man who is strangely noticeable by his absence. For Barnaby and Troy, this is fertile ground for an investigation and, when a second suspicious death occurs, they quickly need to weed out the killer.

Belinda Lang (Elspeth Inkpen-Thomas)

Belinda Lang was born into a showbiz family. Her father, Jeremy Hawke, used to present *Criss Cross Quiz* for ITV and her mother, Joan Heal, was also an actress. One of Belinda's early television breaks came in the BBC's adaptation of

R F Delderfield's *To Serve Them All My Days*, and she followed this with the roles of two sitcom divorcées: Kate in *Dear John* and Liza in *Second Thoughts*. Although she has been seen in numerous other programmes, from *The Bretts* to *Stay Lucky*, Belinda is probably best known as Bill Porter, the wacky, frustrated mum in *2 Point 4 Children*. However, she is no stranger to crime fiction, having appeared alongside Patrick Malahide in *The Inspector Alleyne Mysteries*, playing Alleyne's girlfriend, Agatha Troy. Also, Belinda is married to another detective's sidekick, Hugh Fraser, who played Captain Hastings in *Agatha Christie's Poirot*.

David Ross (Rodney Widger)

One of Britain's top character actors, David Ross has been seen in countless major series with probably the highlights being *GBH* (headmaster Mr Weller) and *Roger, Roger* (hapless taxi driver Baz). Other credits have included *Coronation Street*, *Yanks Go Home*, *Leave It to Charlie*, *Scully*, *Jake's Progress*, *Gold* and *Oliver Twist*, plus a leading role in the play *Eskimo Day*, alongside Laura Howard. A classic piece of TV trivia revolves around the fact that David was also the first actor to play the android Kryten in the space comedy *Red Dwarf*, before the role was taken over by Robert Llewellyn.

Margaret Tyzack (Naomi Inkpen)

When an actress who numbers major roles in classic serials such as *The Forsyte Saga* and *I, Claudius* in her portfolio commits herself to a guest role, it is yet more proof that *Midsomer Murders* is a much sought-after drama among the acting fraternity. Margaret Tyzack starred as Winifred Forsyte in the BBC's hallowed adaptation

'Garden of Death' caught most Midsomer Murders *fans by surprise. It was due to air in sequence with the other four episodes of series four but ended up being screened almost a year before 'Destroying Angel', 'The Electric Vendetta', 'Who Killed Cock Robin?' and 'Dark Autumn', which were shot at the same time. This was the result of late scheduling changes at ITV. A new police drama entitled* Where There's Smoke *was planned for 10 September 2000 but was postponed and 'Garden of Death' was quickly dropped into its place to compete with BBC 1's new drama,* Other People's Children. *Listings magazines such as* Radio Times *were therefore unable to announce the return of Inspector Barnaby on this occasion. 'Garden of Death' did obtain a repeat showing on 5 September 2001 on the digital channel ITV 2.*

*Picturesque
Long Crendon
in Oxfordshire
doubled for
Midsomer
Deverell in
'Garden of
Death'.*

of John Galsworthy's tale of the Forsyte dynasty in the 1960s and was one of the major names on the cast sheet of *I, Claudius*, taking the part of Antonia, in the 1970s. Margaret's other notable credits have been in *The First Churchills*, *Cousin Bette* and *Quatermass*.

Destroying Angel

Story line

Previous page: There are plenty of laughs at the Punch and Judy show, but not for Suzanna Chambers (Samantha Bond) and Julia Gooders (Abigail McKern).

Easterly Grange Hotel in Midsomer Magna is the focus for Barnaby's latest disturbing foray into bizarre village life. He and Joyce attend the funeral of the hotel's 81-year-old owner, Karl Wainwright, a penny-pinching man who has bequeathed his property to his four closest employees, hoping they will carry on the running of the hotel in his traditional backward fashion. Equal beneficiaries of his will are hotel bookkeeper Julia Gooders, chef Tristan Goodfellow, hotel manager Suzanna Chambers and her husband, Gregory. However, on the day of the funeral, Gregory goes missing while indulging his pastime of collecting fungi from the woods. Soon afterwards, his severed hand is found in the undergrowth and the search is on for his killer. Hard-headed wife Suzanna, who stands to acquire his share of the will, is particularly charmless, especially when she presses ahead with the redevelopment of the hotel and reveals she is having an affair with Tristan. Julia, however, seems suddenly racked with nerves and is clearly harbouring a dreadful secret. She gets little sympathy from her solicitor husband, Kenneth, who insists she pull herself together. Yet it is not only the

Cast

Annie Tyson . . . . .Adie Allen	Peter . . . . Gordon Langford-Rowe
Suzanna Chambers . .Samantha Bond	Hilda . . . . Maggie McCarthy
Gregory Chambers . . . .Philip Bowen	Florence . . . . . Caroline Holdaway
Kenneth Gooders . . . . .Jonathan Coy	Ben . . . . Glen Berry
Colin Salter . . . . Roger Frost	Sergeant . . . . Nigel Betts
Tyson . . . . Tony Haygarth	Boy . . . . .Ben MacLeod
Woody Pope . . . . Robert Lang	Junior cook . . . . .Lisa Ellis
Evelyn Pope . . . . . . .Rosemary Leach	Builder . . . . .Jon Rake
Julia Gooders . . . . . .Abigail McKern	Nurse . . . . Shuna Snow
Tristan Goodfellow . . . . . .Tom Ward	
Clarice Opperman .Madeleine Worrall	
Denise Daly . . . . .Niamh Daly	
Mr Bream . . . . Richard Syms	
Mrs Bream . . . . Julia West	
Karl Wainwright . Edward Jewesbury	

Credits

Writer . . . . David Hoskins
Producer . . . . Brian True-May
Director . . . . .David Tucker
Transmitted . . . . Sunday, 26 August 2001, 8–10pm ITV 1

beneficiaries of the will who find themselves under suspicion. Other villagers were in the woods that morning and must account for their actions. Local gamekeeper, Tyson, is one. An angry man whose violent daughter, Annie, is pregnant by Gregory, he points the finger at local fungus specialist Colin Salter, who enjoys naked romps in the woods with his housekeeper. On the fringe of the main action are an elderly couple, Evelyn and Woody Pope. Due to increasing infirmity, Evelyn was about to hand over her prized Punch and Judy show to Gregory but now it seems that her niece Clarice Opperman – whose surly attitude clearly unnerves Sergeant Troy – will inherit instead. Knowing Evelyn's reputation for highlighting local injustices in her performances, Barnaby wonders if Mr Punch might actually provide some leads for the case. But then enters the destroying angel, a fatally toxic fungus that claims the life of one of the suspects and paves the way for yet more gruesome deaths. With villagers falling like flies, Barnaby does not have 'mushroom' for error in his investigations.

'That's the way to do it ...' Punch and Judy lady Evelyn Pope (Rosemary Leach) with husband Woody (Robert Lang).

Rosemary Leach (Evelyn Pope)

Rosemary Leach has graced our film and television screens for nearly 40 years. In the 1960s she starred alongside Ronnie Corbett in the sitcom *No – That's Me Over Here*, in the 1970s gave an acclaimed performance in *Cider With Rosie*, in the 1980s headlined as the Joan Plumleigh-Bruce in *The Charmer* and in the 1990s featured in popular dramas such as *The Buccaneers* and *Berkeley Square*. Add in major roles in series such as *Growing Pains*, *Life Begins at Forty* and *Jewel in the Crown*, and a more recent performance in *Perfect*, and Rosemary's CV becomes even more impressive. Despite all this, she claims her role as Punch and Judy lady Evelyn Pope in 'Destroying Angel' was a dream job, because of her love of murder mysteries. 'I am a real fan – I have a library of thriller books, going back to the first detective stories of Dorothy Sayers,' she declared. 'I also love forensics and if I hadn't acted I would have loved to study pathology. It's the jigsaw puzzle and mystery element of it which fascinates me.'

Tony Haygarth (Tyson)

An angry outsider: Tony Haygarth as Tyson, the gamekeeper.

After a career of prominent supporting roles, in series such as *Rosie*, *I, Claudius*, *Kinvig* and *Our Friends in the North*, Tony Haygarth became a household name when he was cast as Vic Snow in *Where The Heart Is*. Despite this, being a Barnaby fan, he was very keen to have a part in *Midsomer Murders*. 'I love the series because it's charming and has a gentle touch. The Midsomer villages have more murders than New York, but the films are done in a nostalgic style, with a

spooky gothic side.' When Tony met John Nettles at a party, he admitted how much he admired the films. John reciprocated by inviting him to join the team. 'I asked my agent if he could get me on and that's how I ended up playing Tyson,' he says, referring to the cynical, worried gamekeeper he plays in 'Destroying Angel' – another of those bluff working class roles Tony conveys so well.

The Electric Vendetta

Story line

A man's body is found in a corn circle close to Midsomer Parva, with burns to the hands, puncture marks on the lower back and a tuft of hair shaved from the back of the head – classic symptoms of an alien abduction, claims local ufologist Lloyd Kirby. His views divide the village: some locals such as the spinsters Alice and Marion Leonard, who run the post office, and Lloyd's childhood sweetheart, Lady Beatrice Chatwyn, share his excitement; others, including Beatrice's gentleman farmer husband, Sir Harry – the man who found the body – are more sceptical, not to say derisive. Barnaby and Troy fall into the latter camp and focus their investigation on discovering the man's identity and more earthly reasons for his demise. Only days later, a second corn circle death is announced, which leads Barnaby to widen his net and draw in all the likely suspects. There's

a shady character called Dave Ripert hovering around the village and Troy thinks he may have had something to do with a local burglary. Dave's girlfriend, health-centre receptionist Sally Boulter, seems equally untrustworthy, liberally doling out sexual favours to Sir Harry and his new son-in-law, Steve Ramsey, who is already cruelly mistreating Harry's daughter, Lucy. Elsewhere in the village, suspicions are aroused by former diplomat Sir Christian Aubrey and his dying wife, Isabel, who have almost parental concerns for the wacky Mr Kirby but may have a skeleton or two in their own cupboard. This is a shocking case for Causton CID in more ways than one, as Barnaby revels in close encounters of the Midsomer kind.

Alec McCowen (Sir Christian Aubrey)

For veteran actor Alec McCowen, who played retired diplomat Sir Christian Aubrey, 'The Electric Vendetta' provided an occasion for

Cast

Lloyd Kirby . . . . Kenneth Colley
Lady Beatrice Chatwyn. . . Alison Fiske
Sir Harry Chatwyn . . . .John Woodvine
Steve Ramsey . . . . Patrick Baladi
Lucy Ramsey . . . . Daisy Bates
Dave Ripert . . . . Nigel Harrison
Sally Boulter . . . . Amanda Mealing
Sir Christian Aubrey . . Alec McCowen/
Simon Quarterman (young)
Lady Isabel Aubrey . . . Ursula Howells/
Amy Darcy (young)
Miss Alice Leonard . . Merelina Kendall
Miss Marian Leonard . .Charmian May
Michael Rycroft . . . Michael Bertenshaw

Peter Rhodes, Marquis of Ross . . . .
Peter Penry-Jones/
Laurence Penry-Jones (young)
Dave Hedges . . . . .Jonie Broom
Lynn . . . . Eleanor Moriarty
Reverend Ellis . . . . Donald Gee
Driver . . . . .Graham Bill

Credits

Writer . . . . Terry Hodgkinson
Producer . . . . Brian True-May
Director . . . . .Peter Smith
Transmitted . . . . . Sunday, 2 September
2001, 8–10pm ITV 1

what it was called,' he says – and John Nettles, with whom he shared a dressing room at the RSC and also guested in *Bergerac*. Much of Alec's work has been on the stage, but on television his credits have included *Kavanagh QC*, *Longitude* and *David Copperfield*.

John Woodvine (Sir Harry Chatwyn)

One of British television's most familiar faces, John Woodvine has featured in programmes as varied as *Edge of Darkness* and *The New Statesman*. Add in series such as *All Creatures Great and Small*, *Heartbeat*, *Medics*, *All in Good Faith*, *Dr Finlay* and *Z Cars* and he has quite a portfolio. 'On television I have played every rank of

Left: Not such a gentleman farmer: John Woodvine as the devious Sir Harry Chatwyn.

Opposite: The crew overcome the problem of filming in crop circles.

One of the technical problems presented by 'The Electric Vendetta' lay in the need to allow the crew to enter the crop circles and set up the bodies without trampling down the wheat and damaging the design. To do this a location was chosen on the drop of a hill, so that the camera could view across the fields towards the circles and yet be able to hide how the crew managed to get in and out. The circles themselves were made by a man with a piece of string and a crop-flattening board.

The twilight zone: Sir Christian and Isabel Aubrey (Alec McCowen and Ursula Howells) face up to their last days together.

policeman, alternated with "baddies",' he said, adding that 'The Electric Vendetta' allowed him to show off his roguish side in the role of the gentleman farmer Sir Harry Chatwyn who is carrying on with his son-in-law's mistress! 'Playing a love scene at my time of life is an unexpected bonus,' he declared.

Daisy Bates (Lucy Ramsey)

For Daisy Bates, daughter of the late Ralph Bates and star of dramas such as *Forever Green* and *Kavanagh QC*, filming *Midsomer Murders* proved to be a mixed experience. On a night off from production she was mugged and ended up needing medical treatment. 'Unfortunately, I had to stay in hospital and lost some of my scenes,' she said, 'but I got the most amazing flowers from John Nettles and the production team.' Lucky for Daisy, her godmother – Jane Wymark – was at hand to offer some comfort. 'Jane brought me a book and filled me in on the days I missed. My mother met her when she was expecting me, so I've known her all my life and it was great to work with a family friend.'

Who Killed Cock Robin?

Above: From the horse's mouth: could 'whisperer' Sean O'Connell shed some light on 'Who Killed Cock Robin?'

Right: A benevolent fellow? Larry Lamb as Melvyn Stockard.

Previous page: Bloody Evidence – Troy follows the trail of an injured man.

Story line

In the village of Newton Magna, all is not sweetness and light, as Bill Pitman, landlord of The White Swan, reveals to his friend, Tom Barnaby. He's just helped the local GP out of a sticky situation. Driving home drunk from a soirée at the Armsley Riding School, Dr Burgess has mowed down a mysterious man, who has since disappeared, despite appearing to be badly injured. It is thought the man is Sean O'Connell, an Irish 'horse whisperer', an ex-vet with a criminal past who may be up to no good. Suspicion falls on the local squire, Melvyn Stockard, ostensibly a kind and benevolent fellow, but a man Barnaby knows of old to be a ruthless villain. Stockard was with the doctor at the Riding School that fateful evening, in the company of his sultry Spanish business partner, Francesca Ward. The fact that Stockard's former henchman, Jackie Marsh, and his wife are also on the scene is another cause for concern. As Causton CID limbers up for action, a corpse is found in the well on the village green. It is the body of local businessman Robin Wooliscroft, who disappeared some weeks before, having planned to run off with farmer's wife Valerie Megson. This gives both Robin's boozy wife, Bridget, and Valerie's angry husband, Joe, motives for the crime. Now Joe's son is about to marry Melvyn's daughter, much to the disapproval of both fathers, and, intriguingly, the dead man's son, Noel, is to be the best man. Barnaby's brain switches into gear and a complex investigation ensues as he and Troy set about discovering the murderer and the whereabouts of the injured man. What role was played by neurotic former ballet dancer Mary Mohan, outside whose cottage the car accident took place? Or, friend to all, Frank Lightbourne, the village mechanic who offered to hush up the incident? When another murder is committed, 'Who Killed Cock Robin?' is not the only question needing an urgent answer.

Cast

Frank Lightbourne	Mick Ford
Bubbles Stockard	Polly Hemingway
Noel Wooliscroft	Noah Huntley
Jackie Marsh	George Innes
Melvyn Stockard	Larry Lamb
Mary Mohan	Jane Lapotaire
Valerie Megson	Gabrielle Lloyd
Sean O'Connell	Sean McGinley
Dr Oliver Burgess	Ian McNeice
Julie Stockard	Polly Maberly
Bridget Wooliscroft	Linda Marlowe
Bill Pitman	Robert Oates
Lily Marsh	Toni Palmer
Chris Megson	Mel Raido
Joe Megson	Malcolm Storry
Francesca Ward	Yolanda Vasquez
Robin Wooliscroft	Patrick Drury
Reverend Thorne	Jonathan Hackett

Credits

Writer	Jeremy Paul
Producer	Brian True-May
Director	David Tucker
Transmitted	Sunday, 9 September 2001, 8–10pm ITV 1

Larry Lamb (Melvyn Stockard)

Playing characters like Melvyn Stockard – smooth and pleasant on the surface but with a hard heart – is just part of Larry Lamb's repertoire. He's certainly played some tough cookies but there have been plenty of lighter roles, too, in a television career that has taken in series such as *Fox*, *Triangle*, *Get Back*, *Taggart* and *Annie's Bar*, as well as dramas such as *Our Friends in the North*, *Supply and Demand*, *The Wimbledon Poisoner* and *The Missing Postman*.

Ian McNeice (Dr Oliver Burgess)

The lure of *Midsomer* was simply too much for Ian McNeice. Even though he now lives in Hollywood, he was tempted by the eccentricity of the characters and couldn't resist the chance to add his name to the roll call of illustrious guest stars who have featured in the series. 'The characters drew me to the project and I wanted to be among the many famous names who have appeared in it,' he revealed. His particular character, the inebriated doctor Oliver Burgess, typifies Ian's skill at portraying a good-natured bumbler but his acting resumé is impressive and includes some menacing parts. *Edge of Darkness*, *Chef!*, *David Copperfield*, *Hornblower*, *The Cloning of Joanna May*, *Pie in the Sky* and *Conspiracy* are among the highlights.

Above: Under the spell: bumbling doctor Oliver Burgess (Ian McNeice) is intoxicated by the presence of Mediterranean beauty Francesca Ward (Yolanda Vasquez).

Right: Jane Lapotaire as faded ballet dancer Mary Mohan.

Jane Lapotaire (Mary Mohan)

Multi-award-winning actress Jane Lapotaire was grateful for the small role that *Midsomer Murders* offered. Normally taking on far more prominent parts than mousy villager Mary Mohan, Jane was just pleased to be back in work after a particularly nasty experience involving a brain haemorrhage. 'It was an awful time,' she recalls, 'but I'm lucky that I still have my memory. *Midsomer Murders* was my first telly job and I'm extremely grateful to the director David Tucker for offering it to me and giving me the chance to get my toes back in the water.' Jane's numerous previous roles on television included *Marie Curie*, *Blind Justice*, *Love Hurts* and *Ain't Misbehavin'*.

Dark Autumn

Story line

The brutal murder of postman Dave Cutler early one morning leaves no shortage of suspects. Dave has been having affairs with most of the women in the village of Goodman's Land and any of the menfolk could have been out for revenge. Dave's death was gruesome: he was scythed down with a billhook, such as the

one local woodcutter, Ade Jessel, reports missing. Ade suspects Owen August is responsible. Owen is a retired publisher who deceives himself about his standing in the community. He walks the hills every morning while his bored wife, Louise, 'entertains' at home. Also under suspicion is Simon Reason, who runs the local antique furniture shop. He has separated from his snooty wife, Janet, who was another of Dave Cutler's conquests, and he is now secretly seeing Louise. Dairyman Mike Yeatman is also handily placed to be the killer. He works odd hours, is his own boss and has already taken the law into his own hands by beating up Dave Cutler for sleeping with his wife, Mary. However, a second murder, that of attractive secretary/bookkeeper Debbie Shortlands, while her husband, Keith, is conveniently away on business, ensures that this is no cut-and-dried case of retribution for Barnaby and Troy. Their investigation revolves around the two village pubs, The Sword & Sceptre and The Plough, the latter fronted by Londoner barman John Field, who appreciates the quieter life of the country, but whose girlfriend refuses to travel from the city to visit him, even though he has been here three years. His boss at the pub is Barbara Judd, a woman who longs for his attentions. There is a keen rivalry between the pubs which comes to a head during the big Aunt Sally match, in which Barnaby and Troy take part, watched by Joyce and Troy's new companion, local community officer WPC Jay Nash. Yet more murders follow and each time 1950s dance hall music is heard near the crime scene. It is appropriate then that Causton CID have taken over the old village dance hall as their incident room, but, with the killer still on the prowl, the choice of venue begins to seem less auspicious.

Above: Kim Thomson and Nicky Henson as Janet and Simon Reason.

Right: Goodman's Land proves to be a frustrating retirement home for Owen and Louise August (Alan Howard and Celia Imrie).

Previous page: An intimate moment for Troy and WPC Jay Nash (Gillian Kearney).

Cast

Debbie Shortlands	Fleur Bennett
Keith Shortlands	Adam Blackwood
Mary Yeatman	Prue Clarke
John Field	Robert Glenister
Mike Yeatman	Del Henney
Simon Reason	Nicky Henson
Owen August	Alan Howard
Louise August	Celia Imrie
WPC Jay Nash	Gillian Kearney
Barbara Judd	Marian McLoughlin
Janet Reason	Kim Thomson
Ade Jessel	Philip Whitchurch
Dave Cutler	Rupert Walz
Holly Reid	Kate Maberly
Ben Barrow	Morris Perry
Priest	Neville Phillips
Tammie	Rachel Woolrich
Dog handler	Peter Whitear

Credits

Writer	Peter J Hammond
Producer	Brian True-May
Director	Jeremy Silberston
Transmitted	Sunday, 16 September 2001, 8–10pm ITV 1

Gillian Kearney (WPC Jay Nash)

Since hitting the headlines as runaway schoolgirl Debbie in *Brookside* in the 1980s, Gillian Kearney has moved on to star in a variety of prime-time series, most notably *Sex, Chips and Rock 'n' Roll*, *Liverpool One*, *The Tide of Life*, *Hope and Glory*, and *The Forsyte Saga*. As WPC Jay Nash in 'Dark Autumn', Gillian turns Sgt Troy's head and there's more than a suggestion that a long-term relationship will follow. The realities of filming their courtship were less romantic, however, particularly when Troy treated Jay to fish and chips. 'By the time we

The evocative piece of dance music that is heard at the time of each of the murders is 'The Creep', popularized by Ted Heath and other big bands in the 1950s.

came to film the scene they were stone cold,' remembers Gillian. 'We'd had a particularly nice lunch that day from the caterers, but an hour later had to eat freezing chips.'

Celia Imrie (Louise August)

Celia Imrie and John Nettles have a tangled television past. The two were romantically entwined in *Bergerac*, when she played lawyer Marianne Bellshade, but their roles in 'Dark Autumn' are so different there is no prospect of a similar liaison this time around. Celia's role as bright, but bored wife Louise August contrasts also with the numerous comic parts she has played alongside Victoria Wood, and other major roles such as Miss Jewsbury in *Oranges Are Not The Only Fruit* and Joanna Tundish in *The Riff-Raff Element*. One of Britain's busiest actresses, Celia has also had roles in *Gormenghast*, *Wokenwell*, *Black Hearts in Battersea*, *A Dark Adapted Eye*, *The Writing on the Wall* and *Tom Jones* to her name.

Bright but bored: Celia Imrie as Louise August.

Alan Howard (Owen August)

Being a nephew of the great Leslie Howard is always likely to cast a shadow over your own acting career, but Alan Howard has easily managed to garner acclaim on his own terms. Celia Imrie declared Howard to be a hero of hers: 'He is so unusual and I loved playing his wife, which made it a dream part,' she admits. Alan has made a name for himself as a leading Shakespearean actor but his television work is equally notable, with credits in *A Perfect Spy*, *No Bananas*, *David Copperfield* and *Anna Lee*, for instance. He clearly relishes his work. About his 'Dark Autumn' character, Owen August, Howard says: 'I think he is sad, mad and bad. I wanted him to be frightening, arrogant and wilful, like a loose cannon, and in a strange way I really enjoyed playing him.'

The pub featured as The Sword & Sceptre is The Lions of Bledlow at Bledlow, Buckinghamshire, which had previously been seen on two occasions in Midsomer Murders *as The Queen's Arms.*

Tainted Fruit

Story line

In Malham village an old man dies of pneumonia in a cottage which has been allowed to fall into disrepair. The locals blame his 22-year-old landlady, Melissa Townsend, for his death: she has been gifted the property by her wealthy father, so she can learn how to handle money. However, her attitude to the upkeep of the cottage has alienated many, and now, as Barnaby and Troy discover, she has been receiving threatening letters. Even her best friend, district nurse Sally Rickworth, seems to have turned against her. Tensions reach their peak at the local tennis club, where club captain, Adam Keyne, is intent on stirring up trouble, and there is friction between the club secretary, local vet Raif Canning, and his bored wife, Georgina, who'd rather be mixing with the local nobs. Joan Farley, a bitter relative of the dead man, welcomes Melissa by throwing red wine over her pristine white dress. The next morning, Barnaby's old friends, Hugo and Cherrie Balcombe, discover their car has been hit during the night. Along the road is Sally's battered 2CV and she is found still drunk behind the wheel. Faced with the prospect of losing her licence, and thereby also

her job, Sally is distraught, although it is not long before this is of little concern as another body is found – murdered with a syringe shortly after drugs and needles had been stolen from the vet's surgery. There is a wellington boot print in the surgery's garden so the search is on for the corresponding footwear as well as someone who may have been trained in

Cast

Cherrie Balcombe . . . . .Ann Bell
Georgina Canning . . . . .Eleanor David
Joan Farley .Ellie Haddington
Archie Townsend . . . . .Terence Harvey
Raif Canning . . . . .John McGlynn
Liz Keyne . . . . .Sara Mair-Thomas
Sally Rickworth . . . . .Claire Price
Melissa Townsend . . . . .Lucy Punch
Adam Keyne . . . . .Adrian Rawlins
Frederick Bentine-Brown . . . . .Miles Richardson
Hugo Balcombe . . . . .Benjamin Whitrow
Lord Hislop . . . . .Charles Collingwood
Lady Hislop . . . . .Pamela Miles
Derek . . . . .Brian Poyser
Gwen . . . . .Amanda Walker
Postman . . . . .Richard Clothier
Dog owner .Terry O'Brien

Credits

Writer . . . . .David Hoskins
Producer . . . . .Brian True-May
Director . . . . .Peter Smith
Transmitted . . . . .Sunday, 23 September
2001, 8–10pm ITV 1

the use of a syringe. Sally is an obvious suspect, being a nurse; so is Joan, who cares for her disabled, diabetic husband. Joyce, meanwhile, is making medlar jelly and shocks Tom by revealing that the fruit must be allowed to go rotten before it can be eaten. There is talk of a 'meddler' (or could it be a 'medlar'?) behind the problems in Malham and, as the deaths keep coming, Barnaby knows he urgently needs to isolate the tainted fruit.

Opposite: Barnaby and Troy arrive at the murder scene.

Benjamin Whitrow (Hugo Balcombe)

Some people make acting look as easy as falling off a bicycle, as Benjamin Whitrow can testify. For his role as botanist Hugo Balcombe, he was required to potter around on an old bike, looking for rare plants and flowers, but this proved not to be as easy as it seems. 'At first I was given a 1920s bike but it was so old-fashioned that it was impossible to ride,' Whitrow reveals. 'But then I got one from the 1940s which was fine.' Despite the cycling setbacks,

Midsomer Murders gave Benjamin a chance to link up with old friends, especially Ann Bell, with whom he studied at RADA. Since those student days, he has gone on to make a name for himself in numerous TV series and serials such as *Chancer*, *Pride and Prejudice*, *Tom Jones*, *Kiss Me Kate*, *Men of the World* and *Other People's Children*, as well as detective dramas such as *Inspector Morse*, *Jonathan Creek* and *Bergerac*, the last being just one of the occasions he has appeared alongside John Nettles.

Ann Bell (Cherrie Balcombe)

In most people's TV memories, Ann Bell lingers in the guise of Marion Jefferson, the level-headed leader of the imprisoned British women in *Tenko*, a part she played for three years in the 1980s. Her small screen career,

Adam Keyne (Adrian Rawlins) stirs up trouble with nurse Sally Rickworth (Claire Price).

however, has spanned nearly 40 years and taken in appearances in such classics as *The Saint*, *Mr Rose*, *Callan*, *Danger Man*, *The Baron*, *Inspector Morse*, *Blackeyes*, *Medics*, *Agatha Christie's Poirot*, *Tumbledown*, *The Ice House*, *The Woman in White*, *Casualty*, and *The Forsyte Saga*. Less serious parts have come in Carlton's light-hearted rock 'n' roll drama, *Head Over Heels*, and alongside the late Michael Williams in the 1980s sitcom *Double First*.

Ring Out Your Dead

Cast

Hugh Barton . . . . . .Hugh Bonneville
Greg Tutt . . . Dugald Bruce-Lockhart
Dennis Ebbrell . . . . . . .Harry Burton
Reggie Barton . . . .Graham Crowden
Marcus Steadman . Jamie De Courcey
Rosalind Parr . . . .Carmen Du Sautoy
Sue Tutt . . . . Clare Holman
Maisie Gooch . . . . Gemma Jones
Jen . . . . Caroline Lintott
Emma Tysoe . . . . . .Lyndsey Marshal

Judge . . . . Steven Pimlott
Peter Fogden . . . Adrian Scarborough
Angie Blunstone . . . . .Julia Swift
Frances Le Bon . . . . . . .Gwen Taylor
Liam Brooker . . . . . . Seamus Whitty

Credits

Writer . . . . .Christopher Russell
Producer . . . . Brian True-May
Director . . . . Sarah Hellings

Story line

Previous page: Protective boyfriend: Liam Brooker (Seamus Whitty) comforts distraught teenager Emma Tysoe (Lyndsey Marshal).

All is not well in Midsomer Wellow, as Barnaby discovers when Joyce visits the church to practise her new hobby of brass rubbing. There's a right ding-dong over the activities of the village bell-ringing group, which is gearing up for a striking competition that is close to the heart of its leader, Peter Fogden, known to Barnaby as the maintenance man at Causton police station. At odds with Peter is the chairman of the parochial council, former Wing Commander Reggie Barton, who insists the bells should only be used for holy purposes and not for such frivolities. The dispute shows no signs of abating even after the bloody death of one of the campanologists, a renowned adulterer named Greg Tutt whose wife, Sue, had just thrown him out of their coffee shop home. A sinister note left on the body seemingly promises further casualties. Spurred on by Peter, the other ringers – widow Frances Le Bon, her close young neighbour Marcus Steadman, plus teenager Emma Tysoe and her over-protective fiancé Liam Brooker – remain defiant. Other villagers look on with concern: Reggie's drunken nephew, Hugh, parish archivist Maisie Gooch, waitress Angie Blunstone and man-eating lady of the manor Rosalind Parr. Surely they should all be alarmed because no one knows for whom the bell will toll next, or who is pulling the rope.

Hugh Bonneville (Hugh Barton)

Things have really started to move for Hugh Bonneville in recent years. Possibly best known previously for taking over the lead role in the sitcom *Holding The Baby* from Nick Hancock, or as Hugh in *The Cazalets*, he has now won international acclaim as the young John Bayley in the award-winning movie *Iris*, alongside Judy Dench, Kate Winslet and Jim Broadbent. Such credits, however, obscure a varied and prolific career, which also takes in prominent roles in drama such as *Between The Lines*, *Chancer*, *Madame Bovary*, *Mosley* and *The Scold's Bridle*, with comic relief in sitcoms such as *Get Well Soon*, *Married For Life* and *See You Friday*.

Graham Crowden (Reggie Barton)

Stroppy geriatrics and eccentric old bumblers are roles that have stamped themselves on the latter part of Graham Crowden's acting life. Among the highlights have been the wonderfully irresponsible Dr Jock McCannon in *A Very Peculiar Practice* and the subversive pensioner Tom Ballard in *Waiting For God*, elements of both re-surfacing in 'Ring Out Your Dead''s blustering parish councillor Reggie Barton. *The Sun Trap*, *Love on a Branchline* and *Gulliver's Travels* feature among Graham's many other credits.

Above: They shall not pass: Reggie Barton (Graham Crowden) stands in the way of the Midsomer Wellow ringers.

Gemma Jones (Maisie Gooch)

By the time Gemma Jones donned the vestments of parish archivist Maisie Gooch in 'Ring Out Your Dead', nearly 25 years had passed since her most famous TV role. In the mid-1970s, Gemma was a household name as the blustering cook turned hotel keeper Louisa Trotter in the hugely successful

Left: A new friend for Joyce: village archivist Maisie Gooch (Gemma Jones).

Frances Le Bon (Gwen Taylor): the bellringer who is also a crack shot.

The Duchess of Duke Street. After leaving Duke Street, and before arriving in Midsomer, Gemma was also seen in dramas such as *Inspector Morse*, *The Borrowers*, *An Evil Streak*, *Jane Eyre*, *Wycliffe*, *An Unsuitable Job for a Woman* and *Longitude*, but with much of her career spent on stage.

Gwen Taylor (Frances Le Bon)

One of Britain's most popular actresses, particularly in comedy roles, Gwen Taylor proved again that she is equally at home in straight drama with the part of Frances Le Bon in 'Ring Out Your Dead'. Most viewers will know her best as Rita Simcock in *A Bit of a Do*, as Amy Pearce in *Duty Free* or in the title role in *Barbara*, with other major parts coming in sitcoms such as *Screaming*, *Conjugal Rites*, *Sob Sisters*, *The Sharp End*, *A Perfect State* and *Pilgrim's Rest*, and appearances in the Eric Idle sketch series, *Rutland Weekend Television*.

Clare Holman, who plays Sue Tutt, was already familiar to fans of British crime fiction by the time she appeared in 'Ring Out Your Dead'. As Dr Laura Hobson, she was the last regular pathologist to assist Inspector Morse on his cases.

Murder on St Malley's Day

Story line

When Sir Walter Talbot, a benefactor of snooty Devington School near Midsomer Parva, dies in the early hours of St Malley's Day, pressure is brought to bear on his grandson to win the big school race that is taking place that day. Young Daniel Talbot, however, seems very reluctant to oblige, as Tom and Joyce witness on their visit to the school with friends. Sadly, Daniel does not return from the race alive and Barnaby is forced to penetrate the closed shutters of public school life in order to find his killer. At the heart of the intrigue is the highly secretive Pudding Club, a society only open to a select band of boys who compete for a lucrative scholarship into the diplomatic service. Club members include Daniel's rival for the honour, Marcus Heywood, whose sister, Arabella, lives in the separate girls' annexe, while classmate Charlie Meynell, who has been overlooked for membership, is openly dismissive of the club's petty child-like rules. Among the club's old boys are Daniel's father, domineering diplomat Anthony Talbot, and the school's rather ineffectual headmaster, Jonathan Eckersley-Hyde. Other loyal school staff include sportsmaster Martin Fulmer and long-serving porter Ludlow. Down in the village, attitudes to the school are mixed. While its privilege is abhorred, the business Devington brings to the locals is not to be sneered at. Publican Ray Starkey is glad of its trade, as is local cab driver Dennis Carter, who doubles up as the school groundsman. Local youths, such as Ray's son Paul, and Dennis's daughter Julia, are less appreciative of the school's influence, but most outspoken is the local conspiracy

theorist, Dudley Carew, who considers Devington to be the root of all evil. While Troy enjoys the fare provided by school cook Mrs Bosworth, Barnaby, in another sense, has just as much to chew on as he tries to find proof in the pudding.

Jeremy Child (Anthony Talbot)

Whenever an upper-class chappie needs casting, Jeremy Child's name is always near the top of the list, whether the role is to be played for laughs – as in such series as *Backs to the Land*, *Fairly Secret Army*, *Father*, *Dear Father* and *The Happy Apple* – or with a stiff upper lip – as in *The Glittering Prizes*, *Edward and Mrs Simpson*, *When the Boat Comes In*, *Bird of Prey*, *Sharpe*, *Game, Set and Match*, *Headhunters* and many more dramas. The role of devious diplomat Anthony Talbot in 'Murder on St Malley's Day' could have been tailor made.

Ludlow, the porter (Peter Wight) and headmaster Jonathan Eckersley-Hyde (Desmond Barrit) sense trouble.

Cast

Marcus Heywood . . . . Nicholas Audsley
Jonathan Eckersley-Hyde . . Desmond Barrit
Martin Fulmer . . . . .Tom Beard
Ray Starkey . . . . .Eamon Boland
Anthony Talbot . . . . . . Jeremy Child
Daniel Talbot . . . . .Sam Crane
Paul Starkey . . . . .Luke De Woolfson
Charlie Meynell . . . . Thom Fell
Dudley Carew . . . . . Patrick Godfrey
Miranda Talbot . . . . Jane How
Dennis Carter . . . . .Bob Mason
Arabella Heywood . . . . .Anna Maxwell-Martin
Julia Carter . . . . Victoria Shalet
Ludlow . . . . .Peter Wight
Doctor . . . . Roger Brierley
Mrs Bosworth . . . . .Paula Jacobs
George Woodard . . . . . Roger Martin
Sylvia Woodard . . . . .Janet Maw

Credits

Writer . . . . Andrew Payne
Producer . . . . Brian True-May
Director . . . . Peter Smith

Market for Murder

Story line

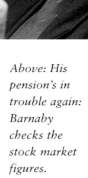

A lucky escape for chauvinistic stockbroker Selwyn Proctor, who is nearly killed in a suspicious car fire, draws Barnaby and Troy into the enigmatic world of Midsomer Market. It is an appropriately named village, as a small group of local women follow Selwyn's example and secretly dabble in the world of stocks and shares, hiding their activities behind the innocent facade of a reading club. However, two of the club seem eager to cash in their profits and when one of their number is viciously beaten to death with a walking stick, and her family silver stolen, their little secret must, finally, be revealed. The investors are, indeed, a mixed bunch. Head of the group is 70-year-old Marjorie Empson, a widow with an uncanny knack of upsetting people around her. Their skilful number cruncher is Sandra Bradshaw, wife of the local GP. She is desperately keen to be part of the social fabric of the village; husband Rupert is less ambitious. Ginny Sharp is the local glamour girl, a divorcée who has a reputation for sunbathing naked and turning the heads of the local men; Lavinia Chetwood is the long-suffering wife of local squire Lord Chetwood, a hypochondriac who can no longer afford to repair the leaking roof on their crumbling mansion; and Tamsin Proctor, wife of the death-defying Selwyn, is trapped in a loveless, childless marriage. Seemingly frustrated at not being part of the group is Vera Hopkins, a meek and mild

outsider hanging on to the coat-tails of village social life, but more phlegmatic is Jack-the-Lad swimming pool engineer Harry Painter, who seems to be in all the wrong places at the right times. Is this simply a case of insider dealing, with death the dividend? Barnaby and Troy need to invest some time in the hope of quick returns.

Above: His pension's in trouble again: Barnaby checks the stock market figures.

Left: In all the right places at the wrong times: Harry Painter, the pool man (Jesse Birdsall).

Opposite: There are shocks in store for Ginny Sharp (Serena Gordon).

Cast

Harry Painter	.Jesse Birdsall
Ginny Sharp	.Serena Gordon
Tamsin Proctor	.Caroline Harker
Vera Hopkins	.Dilys Laye
Marjorie Empson	.Barbara Leigh-Hunt
Dr Rupert Bradshaw	.Christopher Ravenscroft
Lord James Chetwood	.Anton Rodgers
Sandra Bradshaw	.Gerda Stevenson
Lady Lavinia Chetwood	.Angela Thorne
Selwyn Proctor	.Rupert Vansittart
Barman	.Eamon Geoghegan
Police technician	.Jay Smith
Solo voice	.Catherine Bott

Credits

Writer	.Andrew Payne
Producer	.Brian True-May
Director	.Sarah Hellings
Transmitted	.Sunday, 16 June 2002, 9–11pm ITV 1

Anton Rodgers (Lord James Chetwood)

From the mysterious Number 2 in *The Prisoner* to genial cradle snatcher Alec Callender in *May to December*, everyone has his own favourite television memory of Anton Rodgers. His casting as poverty-ridden squire Lord Chetwood in 'Market for Murder' followed years of starring roles, with among the other highlights the parts of William Fields in *Fresh Fields*, vet Noah Kirby in *Noah's Ark*, policeman David Gradley in *Zodiac* and Edward Langtry in *Lillie*. *The Sky Larks* (back in 1958), *Ukridge*, *Pictures*, *Murder Most English*, *After The War* and *After The Dance* feature among his many other credits.

'Market for Murder' tells us yet more about Sergeant Troy. It is revealed that he is a closet fan of The Hawk comic, which he has read since his childhood (much to Barnaby's amusement), and also that he has no head for heights. It has to be assumed that this acrophobia is a new development as he spent several hours in surveillance on top of the church tower in 'Blood Will Out'!

Jesse Birdsall (Harry Painter)

Playing 'The Pool Man', Harry Painter, was the latest of a series of major TV roles for Londoner Jesse Birdsall. His first really prominent television appearance came in the short-lived 'Eurosoap' *Eldorado*, playing snarling villain Marcus Tandy, which he followed up with the part of Government agent Nick Beckett in the action-packed Saturday evening drama *Bugs*. Other credits have come in *The Fear*, *Anna Lee*, *Blind Men*, *Rides*, *Casualty*, *Silent Witness*, *Kavanagh QC* and *Thief Takers*.

Angela Thorne (Lady Lavinia Chetwood)

Marjory Frobisher in *To The Manor Born* and Daphne Trenchard in *Three Up, Two Down* are probably the two roles that are most associated with Angela Thorne, so playing another well-bred lady in the shape of Lady Chetwood would have come as no surprise to the actress who was born in Karachi. Angela's many other credits have included *Elizabeth R*, *Cold Comfort Farm*, *Farrington of the F.O.*, *World in Ferment* and *The Bagthorpe Saga*. She is the wife of actor Peter Penry-Jones and mother of actors Rupert Penry-Jones and Laurence Penry-Jones (Peter and Laurence both appeared in 'The Electric Vendetta').

Not a well man? Anton Rodgers as impoverished hypochondriac Lord Chetwood.

A Worm in the Bud

Story line

Midsomer Worthy is the setting for
this tale of a long friendship turned
sour. Central to the action is historic
Setwale Wood, a tract of natural
habitat that belongs to young
farmer James Harrington. But James
is broke and plans to sell the wood
for re-development. His old school chum, Simon Bartlett, is incensed. A long
and bitter court case has just ended with Simon the loser and James the
drunken, gloating victor. However, Simon's despair is put into context when his
wife, Susan, is found dead in the wood the next day and the terrier-like
Inspector Barnaby begins to scrape away at the personal feuds that dog the
village. It seems that Susan was a source of friction between Simon and James
long before Setwale Wood loomed into the picture, turning childhood chums
into bitter enemies. Their angry relationship contrasts with the calm friendship
that continues between the lads' mums. Victoria Bartlett, proud of her family's
deep roots in the village, is
concerned to see her son in
trouble; her game-shooting
chum, Hannah Harrington,
while distressed at the conflict,
takes a different view and
distances herself from her own
boorish offspring. Other vested
interests in the men's affairs are
held by James's estranged wife,
Caroline, and Bernadette
Sullivan, Simon's barrister-
turned-mistress, not forgetting
Simon's Bible-bashing old farm
hand, Jonah Bloxham, who lives
in the wood. There's also vicar
Edmund Nelson to consider,
whose church, in need of repair,
may benefit financially if Simon
can save the woodland. With
the help of young detectives

*Left: Old friends
Hannah
Harrington
(Gillian Barge)
and Victoria
Bartlett (Wendy
Craig) share a
drink at the local.*

*Opposite: Victoria
Bartlett (Wendy
Craig) helps
Barnaby with his
inquiries.*

Cast

Hannah Harrington	Gillian Barge
Denise Fielding	Rosie Cavaliero
Victoria Bartlett	Wendy Craig
Caroline Harrington	Janie Dee
Edmund Nelson	Ian Driver
Sean Fielding	Charlie Hicks
Jonah Bloxham	Ian Hogg
Julie Fielding	Clarista Hoult
Bernadette Sullivan	Emily Joyce
James Harrington	Adam Kotz
Simon Bartlett	Paul Venables
Sam Fielding	Chris Walker
Judge	Jeffry Wickham
Fireman	Andy Capie
Bus driver	Jeremy Peters

Credits

Writer	Michael Russell
Producer	Brian True-May
Director	David Tucker

Julie and Sean, children of local kennel master Sam Fielding and his wife, Denise, Barnaby goes sniffing for clues.

Wendy Craig (Victoria Bartlett)

Wendy Craig made her name as a stalwart of British sitcom, specializing in harassed mother roles, typified by the parts of Jennifer Corner in *Not in Front of the Children*, Sally Harrison in *And Mother Makes Three* and Ria Parkinson in *Butterflies*. Later she preluded her role as concerned mother Victoria Bartlett in 'Worm in the Bud' by moving into serious drama as Barbara Gray, a.k.a. *Nanny*, a series which she devised herself. Craig has also written under the pen-name of Jonathan Marr and one of her writing credits was for *Laura and Disorder*, a comedy in which she starred in the 1990s. Wendy also appeared in the British version of *The Golden Girls* – *Brighton Belles* – and in the remake of *The Forsyte Saga*.

Above: Junior detectives Sean and Julie Fielding (Charlie Hicks and Clarista Hoult) sniff out some clues.

Right: Can James Harrington (Adam Kotz) repair his marriage with Caroline (Janie Dee)?

Ian Hogg (Jonah Bloxham)

Ian Hogg is undoubtedly best remembered as Alan Rockliffe, the sergeant who was trying to mould a group of raw police officers into a force of capable detectives in the BBC drama series *Rockliffe's Babies*. The same character later moved out of London and began to tackle crime in a rural backwater in *Rockliffe's Folly* – excellent preparation, it would seem, for a visit to Midsomer. Hogg's other credits include the 1975 version of *David Copperfield*, in which he played Peggotty.

Index

Page numbers in bold refer to major entries; page numbers in italics refer to photographs

Major Characters

Allardice, Edward 142–3
Anderson, Doreen 110, *112*
Anderson, Nigel 110, *112*
Angel, PC Kevin **84**, 105, 108, 119, 122, 146
Armstrong, Celia 136, 139
Aubrey, Lady Isabel 160–1, *162*
Aubrey, Sir Christian 160–1, *162*
August, Louise 168–70, *168*, 170
August, Owen 168–70, *168*
Bailey, Ralph 146
Baker, Mr 105
Balcombe, Cherrie 172–3
Balcombe, Hugo 172–4, *172*
Barnaby, Cully 8, 20, 56, 58, 62, 68–69, 73, 77–8, **79–81**, *79*, *80*, 81, 83, *84*, 85, 93, 121, 125, 129, 142, 146
Barnaby, DCI Tom 5–6, 8, *9*, 10–12, 14–15, *16*, 19–20, *23*, 29–32, 35, 40, *41*, *42*, 47, 54–8, *55*, 56, *59*, *60*, 61, **62–3**, 64, 67–9, 73–4, 77–8, 80–5, *80*, *81*, 87, 92–5, 98–9, *102*, 103, 107, 110–11, 114–15, 115, 117, 121, *123*, *124*, 125, 129, 132, *135*, 136–7, 139, *140*, 141–2, *141*, 146–7, *147*, 149, *150*, 151–2, 156–8, 160, 164, 168, *172*, 172–3, 176, 180–1, *182*, 182, 183, *183*, 185, *186*, 187–8
Barnaby, Joyce 8, 20, *23*, 31, 56, 62–3, 74, **75–8**, 76, 80–1, *81*, 83, 93, 95, 107, 117, 121, 125, 129, 141–2, 151, 156, 168, 173, 176, *177*, 180
Barrow, Ben 169
Bartlett, Nurse 136
Bartlett, Simon 187
Bartlett, Susan 187
Bartlett, Victoria 92, *186*, 187–8, *187*
Barton, Hugh 176–7
Barton, Reggie 176–7, *177*
Bayly, Richard 117, 119
Bazely, Terry 98
Beauvoisin, Olive 85, 119, 127
Beavers, Heather 114

Beavers, Ken 114
Beavis, Doreen 125, 127
Beavis, Emily 127
Belgrove, Mr 105
Bellringer, Lucy 91, 98
Bennett, Cynthia 152
Bennett, Gerald 152
Bennett, Jane 152
Bennett, Pru 136, *137*
Bentine-Brown, Frederick 173
Bentley, Nicholas (Nico) 20, 80–1, *84*, 85, 107–8, 125, 146
Bloxham, Jonah 187
Blunstone, Angie 176
Bly, Alice (Auntie) 62, *135*, 136–7, *137*
Bolt, Daniel 152
Bosworth, Mrs 181
Boulter, Sally 160–1
Bradford, Alan 146, *147*
Bradley, Gloria 122
Bradshaw, Dr Rupert 183–4
Bradshaw, Sandra 183–4
Bream, Mr 156
Bream, Mrs 156
Bridges, Fleur 129–130
Bridges, Hector 129–130
Bridges, Jenny 129–130
Brierly, Gordon 142, 142–143
Brierly, Laura 141, *141*, 143
Brooker, Liam *175*, 176
Bryce, Felix 119
Buckley, Brenda 110–11
Buckley, Felicity 110–11, *112*
Buckley, Reg 110–11
Bullard, Dr Catherine 83, **85**, 110, 146
Bullard, Dr George *41*, **82–3**, *83*, 85, 87, 118
Bundy, Mrs **86**, 105, 119
Bunsall, Eleanor 92, *145*, 146, 149
Burgess, Dr Oliver 164–6, *166*
Cadell, Phyllis 98
Canning, Georgina 172–3
Canning, Raif 172–3
Carew, Dudley 181
Carmichael, Esslyn *106*, 107–8
Carmichael, Kitty 107–8
Carmichael, Rosa 107–8, *107*
Carstairs, Henry 132–3, *134*
Carter, Dennis 180–1
Carter, Edie *103*, 105
Carter, Julia 180–1
Carter, Tom 105

Carter, William 114
Cavendish, Jane 125–7
Cavendish, Robert 86, 125, *126*, 127
Cavendish, Stephen 125–7
Cavendish, Tara 127
Chambers, Gregory 156–7
Chambers, Suzanna *155*, 156
Channing, Trixie 114–15
Chatwyn, Lady Beatrice *159*, 160–1
Chatwyn, Sir Harry 160–2, *161*
Chetwood, Lady Lavinia 89, 183–5
Chetwood, Lord James 89, 183–4, *185*
Clapper, Brian 102–5, *103*
Clapper, Sue 33, 103, 105
Constanza, Carla 121–2
Cook, Mrs 114
Cooper, Christine 91, 125, 127
Cooper, Colin 91, 125–7
Cox, Desmond 152
Craddock, Archie 152
Craigie, Ian 114
Cutler, Dave 168–9
Cuttle, May *113*, 114–15
Daly, Denise 156
Dawlish, Bunny 110–12
Devere, Bella 142–4, *144*
Devere, Caroline 141, 143
Devere, Marcus 29, *29*, *140*, 142–3,
Deverell, Augustus 151–2
Deverell, Richard 151–2
Dinsdale, Felicity 90, 129–130
Dinsdale, Tilly 129–130
Dorset, Jack 141, 143
Dorset, Ray 143
Draper, Matthew 127
Drinkwater, Barbara 142–3
Drinkwater, Peter 141–4
Eastman, Brenda 119
Eastman, Ian 85, 117, 119
Ebbrell, Dennis 176
Eckersley-Hyde, Jonathan 180–1, *181*
Ellis, Reverend 161
'Emperor Joseph' 108
Empson, Marjorie 183–4
Evers, Jenny 108
Fairfax, Peter 129–130
Farley, Joan 172–3
Field, John 168–9
Fielding, Denise 187–8

Fielding, Julie 187, *188*
Fielding, Madge 136
Fielding, Sam 187–8
Fielding, Sean 187, *188*
Fitzroy, James *88*, 132–4
Fitzroy, Sarah 132–3
Fletcher, Simon 117, *118*, 119
Fogden, Peter 176
Foster, Mrs 86, 143
Frances, Liz 121–2
Frasier, Iain 125, 127
Frasier, Zelda 125, 127
Fulmer, Martin 180–1
Furman, Rosemary *142*, 143
Gamelin, Felicity 114
Gamelin, Guy 114
Gamelin, Suhami/Sylvie 114
Gibbs, Arno 114
Gooch, Maisie 176–7, *177*
Gooders, Julia *155*, 156
Gooders, Kenneth 156
Goodfellow, Tristan 156
Gray, Agnes 107–8
Green, Mr 108
Gurdie, Ben 133
Gurdie, Billy 86, 132–3
Gurdie, Cathy 133
Hadleigh, Gerald 102–3, 105
Hanlon, Liam 105
Harrap, Muriel 136
Harrington, Caroline 187, *188*
Harrington, Hannah 187, *187*
Harrington, James 187, *188*
Hedges, Dave 86, 132–3, 161
Henson, Dr Barbara 117, 119
Heywood, Arabella 180–1
Heywood, Marcus 180–1, *180*
Hislop, Lady 173
Hislop, Lord 173
Hitchens, WPC 108
Hollingsworth, Alan 110–11
Hollingsworth, Simone 110
Hopkins, Vera 183–4
Hutton, Laura 103, 105
Inkpen, Hilary 151–2
Inkpen, Naomi 151–3
Inkpen-Thomas, Elspeth 151–2
Inkpen-Thomas, Fliss 151–2
Jennings, Charles 86, 117, 119, 127
Jennings, Max 102–3, 105
Jennings, Raymond 114
Jennings, Selina 103–5
Jessel, Ade 168–9
Jocelyne, James 52, **86**, 105, 119

Johnstone, Samantha *91*, 143
Judd, Barbara 168–9
Keyne, Adam 172–3, *174*
Keyne, Liz 173
King, Charles 152
Kirby, Lloyd *159*, 160–1
Lacey, Katherine 98, *100*
Lacey, Michael 98, *100*
Lawton, Sarah 110–11, *111*
Laybourne, Miss 136
Le Bon, Frances 176, 178, *178*
Leonard, Alice 160–1
Leonard, Marion 160–1
Lessiter, Barbara 98
Lessiter, Dr Trevor 98, 100
Lessiter, Judith 98, 100
Lightbourne, Frank 164–5
Lightfoot, Terry 114
Lovelace, Sister 136
Lowrie, Jonathan 84, 146
Lowrie, Marcus 146
Ludlow 180–1, *181*
Lyddiard, Amy 102–3, 105
Lyddiard, Honoria *101*, 103, 105
MacKillop, Charles 146, *148*
MacKillop, Sandra 146–8, *148*
Maddox, Mrs 108
Makepeace, Charles 108
Mannion, Frank *91*, *142*, 143
Marquis, Linda 146
Marsh, Jackie 164–5
Marsh, Lily 165
Marshall, Peggy 108
Meakham, Emily 121–2
Meakham, George *120*, 121–2
Megson, Chris 165
Megson, Joe 164–5
Megson, Valerie 164–5
Merrill, David 121–2, *121*
Merrill, John 121–2
Merrill, Kate 121–2, *123*
Meynell, Charlie 180–1
Millard, Susan 152
Miller, Stefan 129–130
Mitchell, Bill 121–2
Mohan, Mary 164–6, *166*
Molfrey, Elfrida 110–11
Mortimer, Mungo 110
Nash, WPC Jay 70, 73, *167*, 168–9
Neale, Barbara 103, 105
Nelson, Edmund 187
O'Casey, Nurse 136
O'Connell, Sean 164–5, *164*
Opperman, Clarice 156–7
Painter, Harry 183–5, *183*
Panter, Miss 136
Parr, Rosalind 176
Patterson, Gray 110, *111*
Perry, Vince 110
Peterson, Dan 83, *87*, 122, 127, 133, 143
Phillips, Avery 107–8
Pike, Dorothea 122
Pike, Leonard 121–2
Pitman, Bill 164–5
Pope, Evelyn 156–7, *157*
Pope, Woody 156–7, *157*
Prewitt, Arthur 136, 138
Pringle, Betty 133
Pringle, Ron 132–3, *132*

Proctor, Selwyn 183–4
Proctor, Tamsin 183–4
Quarritch, Anne 146–8
Quine, Anna 98
Rainbird, Dennis 47, 53, 98
Rainbird, Iris 47, **98–9**, *99*
Ramsey, Lucy 160–2
Ramsey, Steve 160–1
Reason, Janet 168–9, *168*
Reason, Simon 168–9, *168*
Reid, Holly 169
Renwick, Sebastian **87**, 122
Rhodes, Peter (Marquis of Ross) 161
Richards, Hilary 136
Rickworth, Sally 172–3, *174*
Riley, Tim 114–15
Ripert, Dave 160–1
Rochelle, Jane 143
Rodale, Fred 133
Rokeby, Ava 114
Rycroft, Michael 161
Salter, Colin 156–7
Sampson, Agnes 117, 119
Santarosa, Anna 121–2
Saxby, Muriel 129–130, *130*
Saxby, Will 129–130, *130*
Sellers, Dr 143
Sharp, Ginny *182*, 183–4
Sharp, Mary 98
Shortlands, Debbie 168–9
Shortlands, Keith 168–9
Simpson, Emily 19, *97*, 98
Smith, Becky 108
Smith, John 129–130, *129*
Smith, Michael 129–130, *129*
Smith, Patricia 125, 127
Smith, Rachel 129–130
Smithers, William 136, *138*, 139
Smy, Colin 107–8
Smy, David 107–8
Starkey, Paul 180–1
Starkey, Ray 180–1
Steadman, Marcus 176
Stockard, Bubbles 165
Stockard, Julie 165
Stockard, Melvyn *91*, 164–5, *164*
Sullivan, Bernadette 187
Talbot, Anthony 180–1, *180*
Talbot, Daniel 180–1, *180*
Talbot, Miranda *180*, 181
Talbot, Sir Walter 180–1
Tate, James 146–7
Thorne, Reverend 165
Tibbs, Deirdre 107–8
Tibbs, Mr 108
Toft, Cyril 136
Tomkinson, Major Harry 130
Townsend, Archie 173
Townsend, Melissa *171*, 172–3
Trace, Henry 98
Tranter, Grahame 132–3
Tranter, Kate 132–3
Tranter, Marcia 132–3
Troy, DS Gavin 6, 8, 9, 11, 14, *16*, 20, 30–31, 47, 57, 60, 62–4, 66–71, *65*, 66, 69, 71, 72, **73–4**, *74*, 79–80, 84–8, 94–5, 98, *102*, 103–4, 112, 114–15, 118, 121, *123*, *124*,

125–6, 129, 132, 136, *141*, 146, *150*, 152, 157, 160, *163*, 164, *167*, 168–9, 172, 181, *182*, 183, *183*, 185
Troy, Maureen 73–4
Troy, Talisa-Leanne 73–4
Tudway, Orville *91*, 128, 129–130
Tutt, Greg 176
Tutt, Sue 176, 178
Tysoe, Emma *175*, 176
Tyson 156–8, *158*
Tyson, Annie 156–7
Vellacott, Harry 110–11
Wagstaff, Linda 132–3, *134*
Wainwright, Christopher 114
Wainwright, Karl 156–7
Ward, Francesca 164–5, *166*
Warnford, Dr Clive 136
Watson, Marjorie 'George' 136–8
Wentworth, Angela 119
Wentworth, Stephen 116, 117–19, *118*
Weston, Annabel 143
Weston, Michael 143
Weston, Ruth 143
Whitely, David *85*, *87*, 98, 117, 119
Widger, Marie 152
Widger, Rodney 151–3
Williams, Claire *117*, 119
Williams, Reginald 117, 119
Wilson, Mrs 125, 127
Winstanley, Doris 108
Winstanley, Harold 107–8
Woodard, George 181
Woodard, Sylvia 181
Wooliscroft, Bridget 164–5
Wooliscroft, Noel 164–5
Wooliscroft, Robin 164–5
Yeatman, Mary 168–9
Yeatman, Mike 168–9
Young, Tim 107–8, *108*

Actors and Production Team Members
See also Major Production Credits (p96)

Alexander, Denyse 108
Alexander, Sarah 152
Allam, Roger 110
Allen, Adie 156
Allister, David 130
Anderson, Georgine 136
Anderson, Miles 114
Apsion, Annabelle **126–7**
Armstrong, Moira *26*, 130, 146
Artus, Ashley 114
Asbridge, Nigel 98
Asherson, Renée *97*, 98
Audsley, Nicholas *180*, 181
Ayres, Rosalind 110, *112*
Badel, Sarah *107*, 108
Bagnall, Mark 105
Bain, Derek 14
Baladi, Patrick 161
Ball, Sarah 136
Bardon, John 105

Barge, Gillian 187, *187*
Barrit, Desmond 181, *181*
Batchelor, Dean 152
Bate, Anthony 152
Bates, Daisy **161–2**
Bateson, Timothy **86**, 105, 119
Bayldon, Geoffrey 136, **138–9**
Bayliss, Peter 133
Bazeley, Mark 110, *111*
Beard, Tom 181
Beaumont, Penelope 127
Beazley, Sam 136
Beevers, Geoffrey 114
Bell, Ann **173–4**
Bell, Penny 94
Bennett, Fleur 169
Bentley Productions 6, 12, 14–15, **17–18**, 25, 32
Berry, Glen 156
Bertenshaw, Michael 161
Betts, Daniel 130
Betts, Nigel 156
Bill, Graham 161
Birdsall, Jesse *183*, **184–5**
Blackman, Honor 93
Blackwood, Adam 169
Blackwood, Tilly 114
Bloom, Orlando 143–4
Bolam, James *132*, **133**
Boland, Eamon 181
Bolt, Anna 114
Bond, Samantha *155*, 156
Bonneville, Hugh **176–7**
Booker, Jane 156
Bott, Catherine 108, 184
Bowen, Philip 156
Bowers, Raymond 152
Braid, Hilda 127
Brake, Patricia **146–7**
Brierley, Roger 181
Briers, Richard 8, 21, 60, 76, 90, 92, *116*, **118–19**, *118*, 149
Brittain, Katy 122
Brooke, Paul 110, *112*
Broom, Jonie *86*, 133, 161
Bruce-Lockhart, Dugald 176
Bull, Diane 114
Burdon, Bryan 105
Burton, Harry 176
Byron, Kathleen 122
Cadell, Selina 98
Calder-Marshall, Anna 152
Calf, Anthony 127
Calvert, Phyllis 60, *135*, **136–8**, *137*
Campbell, Cheryl 146, **148–9**, *148*
Canfor-Dumas, Emily 143
Cant, Richard 98
Capie, Andy 187
Carson, Frankie 122
Casey, Daniel 9, *13*, 14, *16*, 17, *19*, 20, 22, 24, *26*, 43, 57, 60, *60*, **64–72**, *65*, 66, 69, 71, 72, 74, 74, 76, 88, 90, 92–3, *102*, 118, *123*, *124*, 126, *141*, 148, *150*, *163*, *167*, 172, *182*, *183*
Cater, John 108
Cavaliero, Gillian 187